The Real Fake

POLIS: Fordham Series in Urban Studies

Edited by Daniel J. Monti, Saint Louis University

POLIS will address the questions of what makes a good community and how urban dwellers succeed and fail to live up to the idea that people from various backgrounds and levels of society can live together effectively, if not always congenially. The series is the province of no single discipline; we are searching for authors in fields as diverse as American studies, anthropology, history, political science, sociology, and urban studies who can write for both academic and informed lay audiences. Our objective is to celebrate and critically assess the customary ways in which urbanites make the world corrigible for themselves and the other kinds of people with whom they come into contact every day.

To this end, we will publish both book-length manuscripts and a series of "digital shorts" (e-books) focusing on case studies of groups, locales, and events that provide clues as to how urban people accomplish this delicate and exciting task. We expect to publish one or two books every year but a larger number of "digital shorts." The digital shorts will be 20,000 words or fewer and have a strong narrative voice.

Series Advisory Board:

Michael Ian Borer, University of Nevada–Las Vegas
Japonica Brown-Saracino, Boston University
Michael Goodman, Public Policy Center at UMass Dartmouth
R. Scott Hanson, The University of Pennsylvania
Annika Hinze, Fordham University
Elaine Lewinnek, California State University–Fullerton
Ben Looker, Saint Louis University
Ali Modarres, University of Washington–Tacoma
Bruce O'Neil, Saint Louis University

The Real Fake

AUTHENTICITY AND THE PRODUCTION
OF SPACE

Maria Francesca Piazzoni

FORDHAM UNIVERSITY PRESS
New York   2018

Fordham University Press has no responsibility
for the persistence or accuracy of URLs for
external or third-party Internet websites referred
to in this publication and does not guarantee
that any content on such websites is, or will
remain, accurate or appropriate.

Fordham University Press also publishes its
books in a variety of electronic formats. Some
content that appears in print may not be available in electronic books.

Visit us online at www.fordhampress.com.

Library of Congress Control Number: 2018947114

Printed in the United States of America

20 19 18   5 4 3 2 1

First edition

CONTENTS

The Real Fake

Introduction

> Welcome to Thames Town. Taste authentic British style of small town. Enjoy sunlight, enjoy nature, enjoy your life & holiday. Dreaming of Britain, Live in Thames Town.

This greeting, on a sign hanging from a medieval facade, welcomes visitors to a charming English village. Everything in Thames Town is quintessentially English, from the Gothic church to the Tudor- and Victorian-style buildings. The cobblestone streets, red phone boxes, and statues of Churchill and Lady Diana offer visitors England at its best. Only one detail complicates the picture: Thames Town is in China. Located in Songjiang New Town, outside of Shanghai, Thames Town is a British-themed village built a decade ago as part of Shanghai's One City, Nine Towns city plan. The plan proposed a polycentric growth model with ten new urban centers, each themed after a European country.

Designed by Atkins, a British consultancy group, and completed in 2006, Thames Town extends over one square kilometer (less than half a mile) and is enclosed within an artificial lake and network of canals. The open-access, pedestrian downtown includes a mixed-use center and residential compounds with five-to-six-story housing. Six gated residential communities surround the downtown area: Hampton Garden, Rowland Heights, Nottingham Garden, Leeds Garden, Windsor Island, and Kensington Garden, the last of which is the only gated area with terrace houses instead of single villas.

Thames Town is many places at once: a successful tourist destination, an affluent residential cluster, a city of migrants—and a ghost town. The downtown area is an important center of the Shanghai prewedding photography industry. Professional photographers capture dozens of engaged couples in a standardized sequence of poses—the romantic proposal, the candid smile, and the happily-ever-after ending. The pictures will be exhibited the day of the wedding, displaying bride and groom in a variety of matching outfits—the fairy-tale prince and princess, Mao's Red Guards, American newlyweds. The engaged couples have become an attraction in their own right, to the point that tourists visit the village to enjoy the extravagant styles of future brides and grooms.

But Thames Town is also a spectral Potemkin village that houses less than a quarter of the ten thousand people it was planned for. Occupancy remains low because most owners had no intention of living there and only purchased properties as a form of investment—real estate values tripled between 2006 and 2012. While the gated communities are about half-full, the condominiums downtown remain semiabandoned. The open windows, hanging laundry, and parked scooters that one sees in these downtown residential areas belong almost exclusively to squatting migrant workers. Employed in the local construction business, these migrants occupy the vacant units downtown. While the residents object to the presence of the migrants outside of work hours within the gated communities, they tolerate the workers in the less iconic downtown areas.

As an Italian architect trained in historic preservation, I was taught to reject the replication of ancient buildings. Mainstream preservation and design theories tell us that the authentic dimension of heritage is neither negotiable nor reproducible. What I understood, once I approached Thames Town, is that those conversations do not do justice to the nuances and complexities of places like that village. The language of "real" and "fake" fails to capture the ways the Britishness of Thames Town triggers the enthusiasm of its users, who both enjoy and construct its atmosphere in spontaneous and unexpected ways. It is the uses people make of it and the sentiments they feel that transform Thames Town into a unique place in space and time. On the one hand, this village typifies the surreal, exclusionary, and controlling aspects that scholars have long associated with themed settings. On the other hand, the Chinese residents and tourists create their own Thames Towns for themselves, genuinely and consciously enjoying the synthetic historicity.

I realized that in order to understand this Chinese-English pastiche, I had to suspend judgment on what was "real" and what was "fake," a distinction that was the inheritance of my own cultural lens. Rather, I needed to look at how the users' ideas of "real" and "fake" concretize in their understanding of "the authentic" and at how this understanding affects their everyday habits and uses of spaces.

In *The Real Fake*, I will argue that the notion of authenticity underlies the physical and social production of space. This becomes apparent in Thames Town, where the themed atmosphere influences the personal and spatial relationships among and within each group of users—the engaged couples, the residents, the tourists, the guards, and the migrant workers. These different groups produce the spaces of Thames Town by understanding, exploiting, and complicating ideas of the "authentic" British atmosphere. The Western appearance of the built environment triggers the enthusiasm of the residents and visitors, who willingly modify their behaviors to enhance their own experience of the British atmosphere. At the same time, the sets of aesthetic and moral codes that residents associate with the English theme marginalize those who do not look like they belong or act "appropriately."

The seemingly antithetical spaces of Thames Town—the crowded themed core; the exclusive gated communities; the vacant units downtown; and the informal gatherings of migrant workers—share a similarity. Their physical and social production depends on how both those who created Thames Town—politicians, developers, and designers—and those who use it—residents, tourists, and employees—interpret and negotiate ideas of authenticity. It is not only that the authentic English atmosphere was fabricated ad hoc to attract residents and consumers but also that this kind of atmosphere influences how people behave. Notions of authenticity, then, underlie the production, consumption, and contestation of all the spaces of Thames Town. Although their uses and users diverge, the spaces of Thames Town are the spaces that authenticity makes.

In using the term "authenticity," I acknowledge and embrace all of its associated ambiguities. The word "authentic" broadly refers to ideas of identity, genuineness, and originality. But authenticity is, above all, about an unresolved tension between permanence and change. We concern ourselves with authenticity when the world that we inhabit changes. As things around us are transformed, we instinctively long for what is gone, though it may never have really existed the way we remember it. It is not a coincidence, then, that preoccupations with "the authentic" emerged in tandem with the socioeconomic transformations of eighteenth-century Europe (Berman 1970). In the last three decades, especially, authenticity has emerged as a potent branding tool to motivate consumers and attract capital (Banet-Weiser 2012). Scholars of urban studies are increasingly aware that the quest for authenticity affects the production and consumption of urban landscapes. People's desire to live and experience "the authentic" in the city underlies phenomena such as gentrification (Brown-Saracino 2009; Zukin 2008), preservation and place making (Jive'n and Larkham 2003; Ouf 2001), cultural tourism and commodification of ethnic neighborhoods (Rath 2007; Shaw et al. 2004), and the Disneyfication of leisure areas (Judd and Fainstein 1999).

Yet scholars have paid little, if any, systematic attention to how authenticity actually functions to shape the physical and social production of space. Taking on this task, I follow the French philosopher and sociologist Henri Lefebvre (1991) in understanding the production of space as a process in which a city's users participate through their everyday spatial practices and emotions. This process involves the physical organization of space as well as the constant arrangement, negotiation, and possible subversion of the social relationships that affect and are reflected in space. In Lefebvre's terms, the "production of space" is an enterprise that involves three simultaneous dimensions: conceived, perceived, and lived spaces. Conceived space is "the dominant space of any society" (38–39) and pertains to the mental and creative constructs that architects, urbanists, and scientists conceptualize and represent through pure symbols and rules. Perceived space corresponds to the concrete environment that people experience in their daily lives through spatial practices. Finally, lived space is the realm of users and inhabitants that includes and expands the perceived and the conceived dimensions. Lived space is the "dominated space" (39) that we inhabit, contest, and construct in our everyday lives. The perceived-conceived-lived spaces, which Lefebvre refers to as the trialectics of space, cannot be treated as an abstract product, endlessly reproducible and equal to itself. Rather, space is an oeuvre, a work that is always transforming and constantly being produced through bodily and emotionally contingent everyday practices.

I interpret urban authenticity as a dynamic relationship between people, places, and meanings that generates urban transformations. As a process of urban change, authenticity underlies the conceived, perceived, and lived dimensions of the production of space. Urban managers conceive spaces that convey dominant understandings of authenticity. Aesthetically edited in order to represent "the authentic," these built environments favor the attraction of capital, establish normalizing sets of behaviors that control the citizen/consumer, and marginalize those who do not look or act in accordance with those norms. The city's users, however, are not passive consumers of these landscapes. They construct their own way of valuing the authentic through their spatial practices—perceiving, negotiating, and at times contesting the narratives of authenticity that are represented in urban spaces. Engaging with the physical and symbolic dimensions of space, city users transform spaces of conceived and represented authenticity into authentic lived spaces.

Thames Town and themed spaces more broadly provide us with the ideal setting for examining these dynamics. Conceived in order to convey a sense of the authentic—although initially of another place and time—themed settings become a stage for spontaneous significations and appropriations. The users of the themed city make use of, attribute, and negotiate meanings and thereby transform the themed, staged sets into unique spaces.

Places like Thames Town are all over China. Entire cities replicating Venice, Paris, and other iconic Western destinations have been erected ex novo. These transplanted cityscapes—which I call "simulacrascapes," following Bianca Bosker (2013)—lend prestige and help market new suburbs. Since the 1990s, the end of the danwei system, land and housing reforms, and the subsequent urbanization boom have made home ownership a symbol of social status. Developers and political authorities have rebranded the suburbs in an attempt to alter the traditional homeowners' preference for the city center and attract residents to the peripheries. Offering iconic themed residential enclaves is key to lure the rising middle class out of the urban centers (Wu 2006).

Most observers tend to ridicule simulacrascapes, associating them with the greediness of Chinese developers, a lack of creativity on the part of designers, and the tastelessness of consumers. Yet the diffusion of simulacrascapes does not imply an uncritical appropriation of Western styles. Not only do rigid dichotomies between what is a copy or an original not apply to the Chinese cultural context (Kloet and Scheen 2013), but many Chinese designers have built themed settings in order to gain the financial security that allows them to experiment creatively somewhere else (Li 2008; Xue 2006). Furthermore, the users and creators of simulacrascapes are perfectly aware of and are willing to cope with their ironies and paradoxes (Bosker 2013; Greenspan 2014; Oakes 2006). Simulacrascapes—their origin and success—thus reveal the specific nuances and contradictions of China's transitions. More broadly, the proliferation of themed residential environments in the Chinese context speaks to the increasing importance of theming in the fabrication of urban landscapes worldwide.

A themed environment is spatially and semantically organized around an overarching motif that evokes an exotic "Other": another time, another place, another culture. The narrative of the theme materializes through architectural features and is reinforced by nonmaterial components such as sounds, smells, and flavors. Although the themes vary according to local preferences, developers and designers draw them from the repertoire of popular culture in order to appeal to as many people as possible (Hannigan 2010). Since the Second World War, the theme park developed as a systematized, reproducible, and standardized model for urban design. With the arrival of Disneyland in 1955, critics, architects, and developers came to see the theme park template as a plausible alternative to the modernist city (Gottdiener 1997). Themed experiences are indeed increasingly part of our daily lives today. As drastic changes have restructured global socioeconomic and cultural landscapes over the last thirty years, cities compete with one another to attract capital. Powerful actors develop formulas for urban growth that capitalize on the semiotics of culture. Exploited globally, the urban theme park growth model materializes in revitalization projects, adaptive reuses, and ex novo developments of ready-made, prepackaged "places" (Bryman 2004).

Most scholars criticize theming, arguing that it produces a fake, exclusionary, and controlling city. Some critics believe that themed settings symbolize "a filtered version of the experience of cities" (Boddy 1992, 124), resulting in a deceptive, fake urban environment (Huxtable 1997). Other scholars focus on how the visual symbolism and built forms of themed spaces control behavior and keep out vulnerable subjects. Disney City's landscapes materialize the fantasies and aspirations of consumers while enabling mechanisms of control that blend consumption, repression, and exclusion (Sorkin 1992; Zukin 1995). The themed atmosphere normalizes certain behavioral and aesthetic codes, implicitly pushing out those who do not look or act "properly" (Boyer 1993; Kohn 2010). The design of urban form also serves the exclusionary character of theming. Corporate themed plazas, for example, are seemingly open to all, but in reality their urban furniture and layout impede specific behaviors—staying for prolonged periods, lying down, or remaining unnoticed—which, in practice, marginalizes specific, disenfranchised publics (Loukaitou-Sideris and Banerjee 1998). Emphasizing these discriminative aspects of theming, most critics have argued that the ordered, sanitized, and phony spaces of the "fake" city impede a "real" encounter with difference and thus the formation of a democratic society (see, e.g., Harvey 1989; Rojek 2000; Soja 1992).

But themed landscapes are more complicated than this dominant narrative conveys. For one, theming is far from a deceptive enterprise. As Umberto Eco (1986) observed, not only are the users of themed settings perfectly aware that they are experiencing a "fake," but part of their enjoyment lies precisely in the conscious experience of the constructed atmosphere. Moreover, as other scholars have argued, the users of Disney City challenge its hegemonic aspects by appropriating its spaces and establishing alternative meanings. At times, people protest the controlling aspect of theming through organized dissent (Warren 2005). More often, users reify, negotiate, or subvert the narratives of themed settings through quotidian uses and tactical appropriations.

Spaces mean different things to different people. Scholars of urbanism have long taught us that we negotiate, produce, and resist the meanings of the built environment by walking, acting, and sensing the city (Chase et al. 1999; de Certeau 1984). Researchers in heritage studies have explored these dynamics, concentrating on how we interpret the meanings of authenticity in the tourism experience. Since the 1970s, they have discussed whether authenticity is a quality that only "originals" possess—a quality thus linked to the material originality of artifacts—or whether authenticity is a social construct that individuals negotiate in relation to their beliefs and expectations. Building on the former argument, scholars in the early 2000s have increasingly agreed that we should understand authenticity not as a finite quality but as a relational, dynamic, practice-related condition that we establish among ourselves and the world around us (Holtorf 2013; Knudsen and Waade 2010).

The spatial appropriations and significations of the users of themed spaces, then, make them into authentic lived spaces, in Lefebvrian terms. These dynamics become especially apparent in Thames Town, where the ways people understand, exploit, and complicate the British atmosphere determine the social and physical production of space. I investigate this process through qualitative fieldwork with four groups of users: the residents, the tourists, the visiting couples engaged to be married, and the employees (security guards and migrant construction workers). I especially look at how users' sentiments toward the British theme influence the ways in which they engage with the spaces of the town.

Three questions structure my exploration: (1) Why do people choose to be in Thames Town? (2) For whom are these spaces open and desirable, and for whom do they remain unappealing or closed off? And (3), when and why do the users of Thames Town follow its script, and when do they break from that script? Observation, survey questionnaires, and interviews helped me understand how the presence of the theme affects users' behaviors in both the free-access downtown area and the six gated communities surrounding it.

My fieldwork revealed that the symbolism of the built environment influences the spatial practices of the diverse groups in different ways. The British theme triggers the enthusiasm of the visitors, couples, and residents, who simultaneously consume and construct Thames Town's unique atmosphere. Although the groups coexist in town, they do not necessarily overlap in their immediate spaces. Only the engaged couples and the tourists mix in the downtown area, where the English theme is most obvious. The atmosphere of the village enhances the playfulness of the couples, who are made to feel like celebrities for a day. The tourists purchase European food and goods to augment the Britishness of their experience.

The affluent inhabitants interpret the Englishness of Thames Town as a mark of distinction and confine themselves within the gated areas so as not to mix with the visitors. The residents play with the core English theme in their choice of home furnishings. Some give their interiors an "English style," appropriating and resignifying Western symbols—Christmas decorations, Catholic items, or British TV characters. Other residents choose Chinese décor. In this, they are motivated partly by nationalistic pride and partly by the pleasure of exercising their freedom to choose—something unimaginable two decades ago—and the ability to purchase in whatever style they like.

The themed atmosphere influences the behavior of Thames Town's users. Visitors, couples, and residents abstain from acting in ways they believe inappropriate. Most residents, for example, avoid hanging their laundry outside to dry—a very common practice in China—to safeguard the "English" atmosphere. Some residents confine themselves to the non-English parts of their houses and leave the English areas untouched, as if they were museum exhibits. For instance, two of the villa owners I met each kept two kitchens in their homes: The open, Western-style kitchen was only for appearances' sake. These residents used their second enclosed kitchens for cooking, feeling that doing so helped them keep the whole house from smelling like food. Equally careful to not spoil the British feeling of Thames Town are the tourists, who refrain from sitting, eating, or disposing of trash unless they find equipment designated for those activities.

The exclusionary implications of theming are apparent in the town. While the residents and visitors consciously change their behavior to conform to and preserve the British atmosphere, the migrant workers are subject to the control and repression of community managers and guards. Most residents and business owners ask the guards to reprimand anyone who spoils the British atmosphere; this policy has the practical effect of marginalizing the migrant construction workers. In most gated communities, the migrants are not allowed to cook, smoke, hang washing, or even sit outside the units they are renovating. Since they are forbidden to make themselves visible inside the residential clusters, the workers gather outside the gates. Some also squat in vacant downtown condominiums, where they are unofficially tolerated and feel less constrained.

Like other Disneyfied landscapes around the world, however, Thames Town is not a space of ubiquitous repression and control. The town's constructed authenticity and the rules enforced to conserve such authenticity also provide the conditions for unexpected appropriations. These appropriations reflect people's desire either to participate in the theme or to avoid the staged atmosphere. Couples who cannot afford to pay a wedding salon, for example, use the sidewalks and streets of the downtown area like dressing rooms. The presence of these informal couples disturbs the managers of the salons, who ask the guards to remove them from the streets. When asked to move, however, the do-it-yourself brides and grooms usually ignore the guards, claiming the right to occupy the street as much as any other (more affluent) couple.

For their part, guards and migrant workers find interstitial spaces, zones in between the most iconic areas, to spend time away from the judgment of residents and tourists. A few guards occupy the vacant units downtown along with the migrants or sleep in the porters' lodge—the one-room structure built at the entrance to each gated area. Some guards also participate in the informal night markets. Despite official prohibition, street vendors and guards sell food and necessities to the migrant workers in front of the gated areas. The gates and porter's lodges, meant for control, thus ironically become spaces where surveillance is loose because the theme is absent and the residents won't protest. Even the spaces of spontaneous appropriations, then, ultimately depend on how different users cope with their own or others' ideas of authenticity.

The spaces of Thames Town exist because the notion of authenticity govern their physical and social production. Developers and designers fabricated the English atmosphere, making Thames Town a space of conceived and represented authenticity. But its diverse users transform Thames Town into an authentic lived space through their everyday bodily and affective practices. Authenticity then simultaneously includes and excludes the users of Thames Town by creating a specific politics of belonging. Ideas of "the authentic" work as a cohesive device when the residents, the tourists, and the couples preserve and construct Thames Town's unique atmosphere through their behaviors. The moral and aesthetic judgments that users associate with the village's "authentic Britishness" also facilitate the exclusion of the migrant workers. But authenticity—the desire to enjoy Englishness, or the need to stay away from it in order to avoid punishment—also encourages contingent and unexpected appropriations of space. The provisional wedding rehearsal rooms on the streets and the informal night markets in front of the gated communities are cases in point.

The ironies and paradoxes of Thames Town reveal how authenticity intervenes holistically in the production of space. The urban processes associated with "the authentic" enable the exclusion of vulnerable subjects, but they equally create unique spatial and social ecologies. Thames Town spaces, and the people who daily shape them, urge us to abandon preconceived notions of "real" and "fake" and to pay more attention to how authenticity makes and remakes the city.

Figure 1. Sign welcoming visitors to Thames Town's downtown.

Figure 2. A couple poses in front of the church downtown.

Figure 3. The British-evoking environment of Thames Town, including Western street names and a statue of Churchill.

Figure 4. Downtown Thames Town's Lady Diana statue, in front of a construction site.

Figure 5. Engaged couples and photographers taking a break during their photo shoots.

Figure 6. A bride getting ready for her photo shoot inside the Lili wedding salon.

Figure 7. A couple, "princess and prince," posing in front of a "French" trolley bus in Holiday Square.

Figure 8. The gates of Kensington Garden.

Figure 9. The residential typologies of Thames Town. From the top, five-to-six story condos in the downtown areas and terraced houses in Kensington Garden include units ranging from 60 to 260 m² (646/2,799 ft²). The villas of the gated compounds vary between 300 and 600 m² (3,230/6,458 ft²).

Figure 10. The green areas between the terrace houses of Kensington Garden.

Figure 11. A teenaged resident of Rowland Heights sitting in the living room of his villa.

Figure 12. The Chinese interiors of a villa in Hampton Garden.

Figure 13. A migrant worker and her grandchild, downtown. They live in the unit under construction and cook on the street in front of it.

Figure 14. "Do-it-yourself" couples getting ready for their photo shoots on the sidewalks of downtown.

I organize the rest of this work in four chapters. Chapter 1 synthesizes the historical evolution of the theme park model and the criticism surrounding it. I especially combine the discourses on theming with the conversations on the privatization of public space. Acknowledging the exclusionary and controlling aspects of themed settings, I nonetheless suggest that the day-to-day activities conducted in themed settings and the attachment that users develop toward such settings complicate the mainstream critiques of theming.

Introducing Thames Town, Chapter 2 explains the production of themed residential environments in the context of China's transition to a market economy. Scholarly conversations on transplanted cityscapes within and outside China prove that simulacrascapes materialize nuanced sociocultural and economic processes. Places like Thames Town, then, cannot be easily dismissed as "kitsch" appropriations.

In Chapter 3, I present the data collected through fieldwork. I describe the specific politics of belonging that emerge in the village because of the British theme. The Western appearance of the buildings and the values that people associate with such appearance inspire the behaviors of all the users of Thames Town, enabling the inclusion and exclusion of different groups.

Finally, in Chapter 4 I analyze the data collected, drawing from the discourses on authenticity in heritage and tourism studies. In understanding authenticity as a relational process rather than as a fixed quality, I argue that authenticity makes Thames Town a unique place in space and time by affecting the physical and social production of space.

CHAPTER 1

The Controversy of Theming

THE EVOLUTION OF THE DISNEY CITY

China is full of places like Thames Town. But Western-like urban forms also flourish in many other rapidly urbanizing regions of the world. From the suburban developments at the fringes of Jakarta, Indonesia, to the new residential districts in Mumbai, India, entire cities are built from scratch emulating London, Paris, or Rome. The global success of styled environments demonstrates that theming strategies help the production and consumption of contemporary urban landscapes. Offering ready-made "places" for the rising middle classes, themed environments sell fast and ensure short term profits to their creators. Although the contemporary transplanting of cityscapes is deeply rooted in the mechanisms of the global economy, the theme park urban typology originated in the postwar United States. Disneyland, which Michael Sorkin defined as "the alpha point of hyperreality" (1992, 206), is acknowledged to be the prototype of the contemporary theme park. Here, I will synthesize the evolution of the theme park model and the criticism that surrounds it.

One might think that theming is distinctive to our times, given the relevance it has acquired over the last three decades. Yet private and public spaces have long featured themed atmospheres. Throughout history, powerful elites created exotic environments for their private delight or to win public approval. We know, for example, that already in ancient Rome the décor of some private dwellings offered affluent citizens the experience of some exotic elsewhere. The trompe-l'oeil Pompeian painting styles are a good example. The same experience was made accessible to the masses on the occasion of triumphal parades, when whole cities were temporarily transformed into staged and themed processions (Favro, 1994). In medieval Europe, the hortus conclusus, an enclosed garden, reproduced Paradise on earth. Contextually, the urban décor of public religious processions made sure to remind common people that Paradise—or eternal damnation—was indeed just around the corner. Later, the most prestigious residences of Russia and Europe encompassed entire villages, where aristocrats and their cohorts could enjoy romanticized pastoral atmospheres. The pleasure garden provided larger publics with the same delights during the eighteenth century. These eclectic assemblages of exotic atmospheres became very popular throughout the United States, Europe, and the colonial world (Harwood 2002; Shenker 2002; Young 2002).

If theming has existed for a long time, its association with mass consumption is a more recent phenomenon, and one that scholars trace back to the rise of the modern leisure industry. The theme park typology has conceptual predecessors in three nineteenth-century architectural genres that combined leisure and consumption: the amusement park, the World's Fair exhibitions, and the department store. The first originated in the United States in response to the recreational demands of a rising middle class. Carnivalesque atmospheres, together with the celebration of technological progress, appealed to diverse clienteles, including women and children (Adams 1991; Peiss 1986). The department store likewise generated great excitement in fin-de-siècle Europe and the United States. For the first time, passersby could admire the choreographically displayed products, walk through sensational architectures, and appreciate the new, efficient retail stores without feeling obliged to buy anything. These private—yet open to the public—marketplaces soon became the symbols of a new consumer culture and its associated urbanity (Clausen 1985; Lerner 2015; Sloane and Conant Sloane 2003). Finally, the World's Fairs that first emerged in the mid–nineteenth century displayed people, objects, and images that had never before been juxtaposed. As complex microcosms, these exhibitions compressed time and space to offer a voyage autour du monde, complete with stereotyped visions of colonial territories and celebratory representations of the West (Çelik and Kinney 1990; Corbey 1993).

Amusement parks, department stores, and World's Fair exhibitions originated in diverse circumstances. However, they had four aspects in common: the construction of a totalizing experience, the accessibility of new publics, the involvement of vanguard technologies, and the primacy of visual consumption. These innovative aspects merged into the contemporary theme park, which is typified by Disneyland (Ottinger 2010; Schwartz 2003).

The opening of Disneyland on July 17, 1955, in Anaheim, California revolutionized the leisure industry, but Disneyland's sociocultural and economic implications went far beyond the realm of recreation. Walter Elias "Walt" Disney envisioned a clean, rigorously confined, and controlled space. Walt's city would be very different from the carnivalesque amusement parks he had experienced as a child. Representing the prototype of a new urban utopia, Disneyland stood as an alternative to both the postwar dispersed city and the messy contemporary urban center (Bryman 1995; Koenig 1994). Disneyland displayed America at its best: traditional towns, beautiful landscapes, and a sprinkle of magic, surrounded by a circular railroad. The Sleeping Beauty Castle, located at the park's center, was the only landmark visible from everywhere in the park. It stood as a symbol of enchantment and reassurance. Main Street, the re-creation of an idealized nineteenth-century American streetscape, led the guests from the park's entrance into its four themed lands—Fantasyland, Frontierland, Adventureland, and Tomorrowland. Inspired after Disney's hometown of Marceline, Missouri, Main Street became a model for designers and architects. Throughout the nation, preservationists brought the Main Streets of small towns back. These architects gave historic towns a pristine condition they had never possessed in reality by demolishing the buildings that did not match with the "old West" narrative and substituting these buildings with authentic-looking constructions. Concurrently, entirely new nostalgic constructions substantiated the collective longing for a preurban Anglo-Saxon America (Francaviglia 1981).

Three revolutionary qualities made Disneyland the prototype of the contemporary theme park. First, the park had an exclusionary character that it conveyed implicitly, through visual codes and access policies. Disneyland's homogeneous visual environment constituted a symbolic system of approved behaviors. Those who did not look or act in accordance with this system were denied access to the park. Another exclusionary feature was the ticketing policy, which required visitors to Disneyland to purchase a single, expensive entrance ticket rather than pay for access to each individual attraction, as had previously been the norm. These aspects, together with the location of the park in a destination reachable exclusively by car—Disneyland was located in a 185-acre extra-urban area close to a highway exit—limited access primarily to middle- and upper-middle-class families.

Disneyland's second revolutionary innovation was to involve the media in both the production and promotion of the park. In contrast to most Hollywood producers, Walt Disney viewed the advent of television as a business opportunity. He built Disney-land in partnership with the weakest television network at the time: the American Broadcasting Corporation (ABC). The network covered part of the construction costs in exchange for Disney's production of the TV show Disneyland, screened weekly on the ABC network.

Finally, the park's third major innovation reflected Disney's ideological confidence in "the ultimate rightness of technological progress" (Thompson 1971, quoted in King 1981, 120). The attractions were regularly changed, reflecting the latest technological improvements. Disneyland's "imagineers," the engineers in charge of creating dreamy imaginaries, developed cutting-edge machines that surprised guests with both the sensational atmosphere and the unprecedented efficiency of the system.

These three aspects of Disneyland's business model—the selection of clienteles via implicit methods of exclusion, the involvement of the media in a mutually beneficial partnership, and the constant search for innovative technologies—revolutionized the amusement industry. But Disneyland also symbolized an innovative approach to urban design, expressed in the Experimental Prototype Community of Tomorrow (EPCOT). Conceived by Disney in 1964 as a fifty-acre residential community for twenty thousand residents, EPCOT would function as a testing ground for new ideas in urban planning. The city was located within the twenty-eight thousand acres in Orlando, Florida, that the company purchased in 1966 for its second and larger park, Walt Disney World.

In the mind of Disney, no unemployment, unmarried cohabitation, public drunkenness, poverty, or even sadness would be permitted in the city of tomorrow. Moreover, since no one would own the houses, the residents would have no voting control (Wallace 1985). The residential community that the Disney Company ended up opening in 1982 is a more cautious version of Walt Disney's original conception. After Walt's death, the Disney Company considered the project too ambitious and converted the residential community into a resort. EPCOT, a kind of permanent World's Fair, is now divided into the "Future World" and the "World Showcase" areas, each encompassing several exhibit pavilions. The socioeconomic implications of the original EPCOT plan, however, resonate into the present (Manheim 2002; Marling 1997; Viladas 1988).

The opening of EPCOT initiated a new turn for Disney. Under the guidance of its CEO Michael Eisner, the corporation created the Disney Development Company in 1985 and became a real estate titan over the following years. Designed between 1987 and 1992 in Osceola County, Florida, the town of Celebration is an example of the neotraditional urban form promoted by Disney. The residential community extends over 4,900 acres on former swampland, surrounded by a green area of similar size.

The designers, Cooper, Robertson & Partners and Robert Stern, emphasized mixed land use, high density, and green preservation to offer upper-middle-class clients a traditional village, complete with a Main Street, an artificial lake, and a marina. Star postmodern architects were invited to design Celebration's civic buildings. Robert Venturi and Denise Scott Brown designed the bank, Charles Moore the Preview Center, Philip Johnson the Town Hall, and Aldo Rossi an office building. The residential areas encompassed condominiums and single houses built in diverse vernacular styles—Disney offered customers a choice among styles such as the "Classic," the "Victorian," the "Colonial," the "Mediterranean," and the "French." The Celebration Pattern Book circulated during the construction process, prescribing buildings' proportions and color palettes. After construction was completed in 1996, homebuyers were asked to sign the Declaration of Covenants, a prescriptive list of behaviors and maintenance rules meant to ensure that the atmosphere in the town remained faithful to Disney's original spirit (Frantz 1999; Ross 1999).

Celebration is one of many traditional urban settings built as an ideological—and commercial—reaction to the modernist city. The sociologist Mark Gottdiener (1997) explains the reasons for this phenomenon by arguing that theming strategies enable contemporary urbanites to convey their social status. During the nineteenth century and at the beginning of the twentieth, patterns of social distinction appeared explicitly in the urban/rural dichotomy, in the distinction between poor and wealthy districts, as well as in the different dimensions of residential units. Gottdiener argues that turn-of-the-century suburbanization processes made this distinction less obvious because location and architectural typologies were no longer indexical to specific roles in society.

As city dwellers demanded new ways to emplace their status, designers began to incorporate symbols that expressed economic and cultural differences into the built environment. This phenomenon became increasingly relevant beginning in the 1950s, when the diffusion of the automobile, the standardization of construction techniques, and new patterns of production created a desire for new modes of social differentiation. Modernist planners did not satisfy this desire. They rather conceived decontextualized urban landscapes meant to actualize values of progress, efficiency, and universality. No space was made to convey difference in the modernist city, where buildings, blocks, and streets looked the same everywhere. Theming emerged as a reaction to this homogenization. With its pervasive use of pop-culture motifs and profound association with consumption, theming defined a new kind of city. This new city, Gottdiener tells us, embodied a melding of material form and commercial culture that continues to this day.

The Disneyfication of the metropolis became a global phenomenon during the 1980s, when the new systems of production and consumption associated with economic liberalization incentivized the diffusion of the themed city (Warren 1994). Andrew Ross (1999) observes that out of the global North theming strategies succeed especially in those regions that experience the advancement of a capitalist consumer economy, the sudden rise of living standards, and a sustained exposure to American culture. Indeed, the political elites and profit seekers of most rapidly urbanizing countries heavily resort to theming. Materializing the pressures of the global economy, styled settings offer growing middle classes ready-made atmospheres for consumption while also ensuring quick profits to their developers (Piazzoni and Banerjee 2017).

John Hannigan (1998) argues that the theme park urban model, which he names "Fantasy City," possesses five central features. It is theme-centric—everything from individual attractions to the image of the city itself conforms to a scripted theme. It is branded—its theme is closely marked by one or a set of corporate identities. It is modular—standard components can be assembled in multiple configurations. It is solipsistic—physically, culturally, and economically isolated from its surroundings. And, crucially, it is postmodern—constructed around technologies of simulation. The development and global diffusion of the Fantasy City has provoked opposed reactions among academics and commentators. As I will show next, while some critics celebrate the themed city, by arguing that it satisfies people's needs, others deplore theming by arguing against its exclusionary implications.

THEMING AND FAKENESS

Theming is a polarizing practice. Since the opening of Disneyland, critics have discussed the socioeconomic and cultural implications of the urban theme park model. Their reactions tend to converge on two arguments. Some observers respond enthusiastically to Disney's city. They argue it provides the kind of space that people want and that architects and planners have long neglected. Other commentators remain critical of theming, contending that it inevitably produces a fake, exclusionary, and controlling city. These scholars link the production of themed settings to problematics of hegemony, privatization, and authenticity. In the scholarly conversation around theming, authors tend to attribute the defense of theming to commentators in the professional fields—architects, designers, or journalists—and ascribe a more critical perspective to academic inquirers. This view, I would suggest, implicitly trivializes the arguments in favor of theming. It assumes that the observations of those who favor styled milieus are driven by practical considerations and lack the depth and intellectual sophistication of those who are critical. In this section, I hope to demonstrate that the debates surrounding the ethics, politics, and meaning of theming reveal nuanced interpretations on both sides.

There have long been theming enthusiasts in both the professional and academic worlds. In his keynote speech at the 1963 Urban Design Conference at Harvard, the real estate developer James W. Rouse defined Disneyland as "the greatest piece of urban design in the United States" (quoted in Marling 1997, 170). He argued that the standards of the park in terms of design, popular success, and technological advancement should be a model for architects and planners. Rouse's lesson has been taken up by organizations such as the Urban Land Institute, the American Planning Association, and—of course—the Themed Entertainment Association, which have assisted professionals and researchers in interpreting, designing, and managing themed settings (Hannigan 1998). While these institutions are primarily motivated by profit, scholars have praised the Disney city on more theoretical grounds. The world-famous architect Charles Moore argued in 1972, for example, that Disneyland recreated "all the chances to respond to a public environment" that had disappeared in the modernist and sprawl models. According to Moore, Disneyland allowed interaction and participation. It "created a place" by providing a "whole public world, full of sequential occurrences, of big and little drama, full of hierarchies of importance and excitement." To those who objected that the park was, in fact, private and expensive to enter, Moore replied: "Curiously, for a public place, Disneyland is not free. You buy tickets at the gate. But then, Versailles cost someone a great deal of money, too. Now, as then, you have to pay for the public life" (2004 [1972], 126).

The excitement for the urban theme park model increased even further after the opening of Disney World in 1971. The architect and critic Peter Blake, for example, described the new park as "the most interesting New Town in the United States." Considering the disastrous effects of modernism, Blake suggested that Disney's city offered a valiant alternative to most recent design trends and that "urban men might, just possibly, be saved by a mouse." The academic and architect Robert Venturi equally praised the qualities of Disney parks, which in his opinion were "nearer to what people really want than anything architects have ever given them" (Goldberger 1972, 42). The sixth Venice Architecture Biennale assigned Disney a place in the landscapes of high culture in 1966, when the US pavilion celebrated the architecture of Disney by featuring the work of over thirty famous designers.

This was the period in which postmodern architects were reclaiming the use of décor that their predecessors had banned. In the view of postmodern critics, featuring buildings with aesthetically pleasing elements would give the city back to its legitimate owners: the people. Postmodern designers rejected the abstract, aseptic, and technocratic modernist city. They wanted to make architecture communicate meanings to its users, as it had in the past. Historical and stylistic elements were no longer to be banned, but postmodernists used them to decorate buildings, piazzas, or even entire cities with references that people could identify. Theming was then seen as a democratizing practice that would reconnect the city to its populace (Jencks 1977; Rossi 1990). Corporate logic soon domesticated the criticality of postmodernism. Obtaining little public funding, architects turned to private sponsors to implement their creativity. Disney, a company with commissioning power that exceeded that of some nations and that also held a consuming interest in the inventive re-creation of history, became the ideal client of major "arch-stars" (Ross 1999).

Progressive critics labeled postmodernism "the architecture of Reaganism," contesting its profitable relationship with corporate clients. These observers argued that postmodern city planning, and themed settings as its emblem, materialized capitalism at its worst by exacerbating inequalities. Rather than democratizing space, theming was found guilty of producing consumption clusters that left out all those who could not afford to enter them (Boyer 1993; McLeod 1989). The supporters of theming in turn charged progressive critics of maintaining elitist attitudes. The architecture critic Paul Goldberger (1989), for example, urged architects and planners to embrace realism and accept the death of the public realm as they knew it. In Goldberger's view, designers were to acknowledge that no grand vision could make contemporary urban problems disappear. Professionals should work from within the system rather than seeking to dismantle it—an operation that had persistently proved fallacious. Architects had to improve people's lives while dealing with realistic constraints. This, Goldberger argued, implied accepting that functional public spaces could be built, but under the auspices of private investments. In line with Goldberger's argument, the supporters of Disney's city continue to insist that antitheming feelings reveal an elitist mindset. Most intellectuals, they argue, condemn themed settings without considering that their popular success also determines the democratization of city spaces (Lowenthal 2002; Lukas 2013).

Yet we cannot dismiss the critiques of theming by simply arguing that it gives people "what they like." The fantasy city does raise issues of exclusion, authenticity, and control. Exploring these circumstances, scholars employ their critique of theming around three interrelated issues: hyperreality, symbolic consumption, and hegemonic control. Critics who focus on the hyperreal character of themed settings speculate on the implosion of time and space in postmodern societies and argue that distinctions between original and artifice inform less and less of our understanding of the world (Baudrillard 1983, 1994; Eco 1986; Harvey 1990; Jameson 1991; Soja 1989). Those who link theming practices to symbolism explore how consumption and production are increasingly intertwined in the experience economy (Gilmore and Pine 1999). We know that powerful actors foster city branding to attract capital (Lang 2011). Cities must at once reassure and enchant citizens/consumers in order to compete with one another in the global arena. To this end, institutional and private actors ensure homogenous patterns in the delivery of goods and services while also luring consumers with totalizing, emotional, and symbolical-ly evocative urban experiences (Bryman 2004; Klingmann 2007; Ritzer 1999, 2003). Finally, critics who speculate on the antidemo-cratic aspects of theming refer to hegemonic control as the process by which power is obtained via the agency of persuasion instead of coercion. In a hegemonic regime, power actors reach consent by engaging in constant negotiation with subordinated groups and appealing to their common sense to exert control (Gramsci 1977 [1929]).

Speculating on issues of hyperreality, symbolic consumption, and hegemony, scholars associate theming with an inauthentic and exclusionary city. Critics who focus on the "fakeness" of themed settings usually combine discussions of hyperreality and symbolic consumption. As technologies allow the perfect repro-duction of objects and places, they equally enable a new condition of proximity and propinquity between people and places. Scholars have observed that in this scenario the design of the urban form is increasingly detached from local socioeconomic and cultural con-texts (Arefi 1999; Auge 1995). Themed environments typify the detachment between indigenous needs and global forces of profit. In his now classic treaty on the theme park urban model, Michael Sorkin (1992) criticizes theming by arguing that it produces an "a-geographical city" that simultaneously erases and produces dif-ferences. The new "non-place urban realm" of the themed city at once loses ties to any specific space and re-creates them through the invention of a "universal particular" (Sorkin 1992, xii).

Scholars have long criticized the a-geographical character of themed settings. Detached from any locality, the city of simulation gives publics "the sinister impression of kitsch, retro, and porno at the same time" (Baudrillard 1994, 38). The geographer Edward Soja (1992) named the urban system that derives from these pro-cesses "Exopolis." As the city that lost its "cityness," Exopolis merges real and fake in prepackaged and security-obsessed forms and denies any form of organic urbanity that had existed before. Separated from the rest of the urban fabric, Exopolis provides "a filtered version of the experience of cities, a simulation of urban-ity" (Boddy 1992, 124). The customization of history and geography is central to the theme park city. To transform the past into an easily digestible commodity, designers simplify historical periods and geographical regions so to make them recognizable in the décor of themed settings (Wallace 1985). The architecture critic and Pulitzer Prize winner Ada Louise Huxtable (1997) particularly concerned with the "fakeness" of themed settings. She argued that the theme park model, which in her view increasingly typified the American city, overturned the relationship between reality and fantasy, resulting in a deceptive and fake urban environment.

But theming is far from a deceptive practice. As Umberto Eco noted long ago, the users of themed settings are perfectly aware of their lack of originality. The Italian philosopher recalled a revelatory memory of his own discovery of themed America and used it to argue that the emotional involvement toward spaces and objects transcends their realness or fakeness. In the experience of themed settings, "falsehood is enjoyed in its fullness," and the authenticity of objects is "essentially a visual property" (Eco 1986, 40).

Categories of realness and fakeness, therefore, do not really matter in the users' experience of themed environments. This becomes especially apparent in historical theme parks. Scholars have long argued that the visitors of most re-created heritage sites appreciate the pastness that the atmosphere conveys independently from whatever material authenticity the toured scene conserves (Cohen 1988; Pearce and Moscardo 1986). An excellent example is the global success of "time traveling"—the practice of dressing and acting in order to reproduce specific historical moments. This practice allows individuals to experience and enjoy a sense of the past that has nothing to do with the age value of the artifacts around them (Holtorf 2009). Other scholars emphasize that the users of themed settings not only know that the space is not authentic in its material components, but they appreciate the space precisely because of its fakeness. Indeed, in most cases people visit themed environments especially willing to appreciate their staged ambience. Building on this consideration, researchers have proved that the success of styled restaurants, museums, and heritage sites heavily depends on the degree to which these environments convincingly re-create the atmosphere they have promised (Beardsworth and Bryman 1999; Lukas 2013).

THEMING AND EXCLUSION

We might thus concede that, as Eco argued, the "fakeness" of themed settings should not concern us from an ethical perspective—users appreciate the space precisely because of its ability to convey a fabricated atmosphere. But if the deceptive qualities of themed settings can be debated, their exclusionary and controlling aspects cannot. Theming strategies marginalize vulnerable groups through both explicit and implicit methods. Those who are left out from themed environments are the individuals who cannot afford to consume enough, or whose very presence inhibits others' will to consume. These dynamics are sadly familiar to scholars concerned with the privatization and securitization of public space.

Increased surveillance and privatization intersect with the fragmentation of the public sphere. Scholars have lamented this phenomenon since the 1970s, arguing that public space has lost its traditional qualities of trust, openness, freedom of speech, and diversity (Davis 1990; Sennett 1970, 1977). This narrative of loss has been criticized especially since the 1990s, when scholars argued that mourning public space both romanticizes its original qualities and overlooks the everyday practices that subvert normative categories of urban life (Carmona 2010). On the one hand, stories of how the public is not public anymore simply ignore that "public" was never truly public in the first place. Feminist scholars especially insist that those who criticize the loss of public space ignore that throughout history only very few people—namely wealthy white men—could actually access public spaces and participate in political life (Fraser 1990; Young 1989). Other scholars have pointed out that superficial encounters among strangers do not necessarily lead to mutual respect. For this reason, we should not idealize the democratizing qualities of public space, nor should we assume that its very existence will resolve systemic injustices (Amin 2008).

On the other hand, scholars have argued that the narrative of the loss of public space overlooks that everyday practices socially and physically construct a city. Michel de Certeau (1984) taught us that people alter spaces around them through their quotidian practices. With some similarities to Lefebvre's trialectics of space, Certeau suggested that a city's users contest the "strategies" imposed by governments and corporations by emplacing situated "tactics" that resist dominance. Using and signifying what surrounds us, we thus reify, negotiate, and possibly subvert prescribed behaviors. Scholars have built on this consideration, arguing that different individuals, especially the most vulnerable among a city's users, disrupt normative categories of urban space by appropriating the city in spontaneous ways. In doing so, they claim a "Right to the City" (Lefebvre 1996 [1968]) and force us to rethink notions of political participation and citizenship (Crawford 1995, 1999; Purcell 2003).

We should not, then, equate public space with increased justice. However, we should remember that the coexistence among strangers in public spaces can facilitate acceptance of Others. In overlapping in space and seeing one another, different people get used to diversity and develop a positive indifference toward strangers, if not convivial relationships with them (Anderson 2011; Peattie 1999). Increasing privatization and securitization do have vicious consequences because they impede encounters among different groups and thus prevent people from normalizing difference in the city (Loukaitous-Sideris 2012; Madanipour 2006). For this reason, scholars insist, planners and designers should actively engage in preserving and creating public spaces that not only accept but celebrate difference as constitutive of the urban experience (Fincher 2003; Sandercock 1998).

The aesthetic and spatial qualities of themed environments hinder the safeguard of public space and thus have exclusionary consequences. The association of theming with the privatization of public space is long established. Developers worldwide use the theme park urban model in revitalization projects, adaptive reuses, and ex novo developments. These projects materialize our aspirations for a good, safe-yet-exciting, and "authentic" life. They also, however, typify mechanisms of control that blend consumption, repression, and exclusion (Zukin 1995, 2010). Michael Sorkin indicates that one of the characteristics of "Disney City" is its "obsession with security," which leads to rising levels of "surveillance over its citizenry" and enhances the "proliferation of new modes of segregation" (1992, xv). His preoccupations echo the frequent argument that fortified, themed enclaves have replaced public space with private surrogates (see, e.g., Harvey 1989; Rojek 2000). Indeed, the "invented streets" of the themed city offer all the comforts and none of the risks of traditional urban fabrics. The designers and managers of Disney City make sure that its users/consumers remain undisturbed by the encounter with difference (Banerjee 2001). Christine Boyer (1993) argues that spectacular themed environments are part of an independent urban system that she terms the "City of Illusion." This independent urban system runs parallel to the territories in which it is located. Themed environments might seem to offer equal possibilities to all. Yet, of course, the "equals" who can access the City of Illusion are only those who have real purchasing power. Themed environments, in fact, form separate arrangements of leisure and consumption that extrude and displace the poor (Boyer 1993).

Theming strategies imply the exclusion of a city's "undesirables" (Whyte 1999) in multiple ways. They explicitly segregate when users must pay to access themed environments, when employees are requested to maintain a particular appearance, or when entrance is granted only to people of a specific age or origin. But the themed city also—and especially—operates through subtle techniques. One technique is the establishment of commonsensical norms that tell people how they should look and act. Powerful institutions have long exerted control over people by imposing visual and behavioral codes. Throughout history, access to certain spaces was explicitly forbidden to specific kinds of people. In colonial Shanghai, for example, Chinese populations were usually forbidden entrance to public parks (Bickers and Wasserstrom 1995). Since the 1960s, the battles for civil rights in the global North and the rise of indigenous movements in former colonial territories have changed the ways authorities regulate the uses of the city. As laws that precluded specific groups from using spaces progressively disappeared, urban managers found more subtle ways to zone out the poor, the immigrant, and the homeless from a city's prime spaces. Rather than explicitly punishing people, municipal rules now punish "improper" behaviors. These rules de facto exclude vulnerable groups by targeting those individuals who are more likely to engage in forbidden behaviors. By preventing people from standing in the street for a prolonged time, for example, authorities target beggars, the homeless, and street vendors (Blomeley 2007; Cross and Morales 2007; Kim 2015).

Urban design serves the exclusionary character of theming. Staged spaces are designed to control users by regulating four aspects of agency: desire, consumption, movement, and time. Marketing strategies stimulate desire and consumption, while the physical components of the space regulate people's uses of time and space (Judd 1999, 2003). Corporate "public" spaces, which are often themed, are an excellent example. Seemingly open to all, these spaces make it very hard—if not impossible—for people to stay more than a couple of hours in the same place. The benches are not comfortable to sit on for longer than twenty minutes, and armrests prevent users—the homeless—from lying down. Access to these spaces can become complicated if you are not fit or are carrying something. A shopping cart can hardly be transported over the stairs of a plaza, for example. The spatial layout of the corporate plaza ensures that everybody remains visible. No sheds, bushes, or partitions are big enough to allow someone to hide in or behind them. At night, these spaces are flooded with light to make sure that no one can sleep. Studded with surveillance cameras, corporate plazas resemble panoptical experiments. Those who "have nothing to hide" from city officials feel safe and comfortable. The others, the "undesirables," feel unsafe and remain excluded (Banerjee and Loukaitou-Sideris 2013; Loukaitou-Sideris and Banerjee 1998).

The symbolism of themed spaces both influences people's behaviors and keep distant those who do not look "proper." Theme parks satisfy and re-create consumers' longing for the lifestyles they represent (Davis, 1996). In her seminal work on the "landscapes of power," Sharon Zukin dedicates particular attention to the exclusionary implications of themed settings. Stage-set landscapes, she argues, project the fantasies of the powerless while hegemonically imposing social and cultural standards. Styled environments then function as "liminal" spaces, spaces at the edges, in between "nature and artifice, and market and place" (Zukin 1991, 231). These liminal areas attract visitors because they stand as safe and aesthetically appealing places different from the rest of the urban fabric. Zukin argues that through their alleged uniqueness themed settings reorganize space and time, reformulate economic roles, and revalue cultures of production and consumption.

The form and look of styled settings influences how people behave. Scholars have long acknowledged the power of visuality in establishing territorial control. Throughout history, physical and cultural landscapes have reflected logics of power (Cosgrove 1985). Judgments on who belongs to a place and who is instead "out of place" become naturalized within sociocultural contexts (Cresswell 1996). The built environment—its shape, materials, and aspect—conveys ideas of the "proper" to its users (Dovey 2010). This becomes particularly evident in the case of themed settings, where powerful actors exploit the semiotics of space to suggest and impose meanings and conducts (Gottdiener 1985). The aesthetic qualities of themed settings actively keep distant nondesirable customers. Conveying ideas of the "out of place," theming segregates those individuals who do not belong to the scene. Vulnerable subjects then tend to avoid these flashy, crafted, securitized bubbles of consumption, where it is hard for them to remain unnoticed. Thames Town is a case in point. As I will argue in Chapter 3, the presence of the theme affects the ways people behave as they seek to conform and create ideas of authentic "Britishness." Moreover, Thames Town's appearance also makes the presence of the migrant workers' stand as the "out of place," effectively discouraging these users from occupying the most iconic village areas.

Themed settings prevent diverse people from interacting or seeing one another. The lack of visual and physical contact between heterogeneous groups has alienating social effects on all groups. Scholars have long argued that the encounter with difference in the city is essential to personal and collective growth (Fincher and Jacobs 1998; Friedman and Douglass 1998). Margaret Kohn (2010) suggests that privatization processes, and corporate themed clusters as their emblem, impede publics from forming political consciousness. Preventing access to underprivileged groups, themed settings are only used by individuals of similar backgrounds. Themed privatized clusters are "social spaces" in that they allow people to enact sociability—superficial exchanges among peers—but are not public spaces because they do not enable an encounter with difference. This lack of contact prevents a city's users from both accepting the existence of strangers and understanding their role within societies via comparison with others. Kohn's nuanced conclusions encapsulate the much-rehearsed critique that the Disneyfied city obstructs democracy. Most critics indeed argue that while "real" public spaces allow individuals to develop a civic consciousness, the "fake" public spaces of the themed city impede the formation of a democratic polity (e.g., Harvey 1990; Rojek 2000; Soja 1992).

Themed landscapes, however, are more complicated than this narrative suggests. While the producers of the Disneyfied city fabricate dominant values of the proper, its users reify and possibly contest such values through their everyday activities. As Sharon Zukin (1995) suggests, we should not only acknowledge the dominant mechanisms that create cities, but we should also and foremost unveil the dynamics that challenge the hegemonies of urban landscapes. Attention must be paid to how the ordinary practices and emotions of a city's users socially and physically produce space. Building on this consideration, Stacey Warren has explored how institutions and users resist dominance in themed settings. Warren argues that the Disneyfied city is truly hegemonic because as much as it materializes top-down dynamics it also incorporates resistance from within. The spaces of the Disneyfied city work as hegemonic possibilities "inserted into the urban fabric and experienced by real people" (Warren 2005, 254). We cannot assume that those who are officially in control of a city are the only ones who participate in the social production of space. Individuals resist top-down city making through organized dissent. As an example of this phenomenon, Warren (1999, 2005) analyzes how local groups and some of their political representatives contested and ultimately changed Disney's plans in Seattle, Long Beach, Anaheim, and Haymarket in Virginia.

The users of themed settings also express their concerns, fabricate meanings, and establish new norms through their day-to-day practices. We know that spatial arrangements embody the local habitus. The members of a social group assimilate norms, behaviors, and expectations that they take for granted when interacting with one another and in space (Bourdieu 1979). We are also familiar, however, with the fact that, through everyday social and spatial habits, users reinvent the city and discover new opportunities to live in it (Crawford 1999; Certeau 1984). Researchers in tourism have linked discourses on the everyday with conversations on authenticity. They have proved that not even the staged enclaves of the most visited destinations remain exempt from the disorder, messiness, and unpredictability typical of less crafted cities (Bagnall 1996, 2003). Tourists experience the city in different ways through their bodily and affective practices. Through their experience of place, they challenge the existence of a single, dominant narrative of "the authentic" (Knudsen and Waade 2010; Rickly-Boyd 2013; Zhu, 2012).

Disneyfied citadels of consumption do not necessarily remain spaces of absolute control. They get reinvented and resisted each time their users produce alternative narratives of meanings. John Fiske (1989) famously distinguished the "cultural products" that capitalist societies make from "popular culture," which describes the ways in which people actually use and understand such products by creating their own meanings. Fiske looked at how groups of young people experienced Australian shopping malls and found that they used these spaces in ways very different from what they were created for. Unemployed youth with no purchasing power turned shopping malls into their meeting places and "tricked" security guards by putting alcohol in soda cans. Analyzing these subversive practices, Fiske concluded that shopping malls are where the "strategy of the powerful is most vulnerable to the tactical raids of the weak" (2000, 325). Contestations also take place into residential themed clusters. In Celebration, the residents consciously negotiate the paradoxes of living in Mickey Mouse's town. Steve Ross (1999) reports that residents contested some rules of the Celebration Pattern Book by arguing that they limited the dwellers' freedom to design exteriors as they liked.

Celebration's residents changed the rules by both convincing the city to modify regulations and by transforming the built environment on their own. Moreover, Celebration's residents also learned to perform different roles for different audiences. When speaking to journalists, for example, residents emphasize enthusiastic feelings that do not mirror their real sentiments toward the town. They consciously decide to perform the part they know media representatives want them to play, keeping their more nuanced reflections to themselves.

The exclusionary character of theming remains unquestionable. The managers of the Disneyfied city filter and condition their clienteles through the design of space and by imposing visual and behavioral codes. These measures influence the ways in which people use the space. They also inhibit access to those who do not look or act as if they belong in the bounded spaces of consumption. However, the everyday spatial and affective practices of the users constantly refabricate and possibly contest the meanings of themed settings. The users of the Disneyfied city consciously experience its fakeness and at times subvert its controlling aspects. These circumstances complicate the claim that the themed city has left its residents hopeless. All this becomes apparent in Thames Town, where the visitors, residents, and workers experience the village in unexpected ways.

CHAPTER 2

Thames Town and the Chinese Landscapes of Mimicry

THAMES TOWN: A BRITISH VILLAGE IN SHANGHAI

Built under the auspices of Shanghai's One City, Nine Towns city plan (2001–2005), Thames Town is an ideal site in which to investigate the social implications of theming. Enclosed within an artificial lake and network of canals, the village is comprises one square kilometer and includes a mixed-used downtown surrounded by six residential gated communities.

Thames Town was completed in three years, with the typical urgency of Chinese urbanization processes. Yet the eclectic built environment imitates the natural stratification of a real historic urban fabric, including a Gothic church, Victorian residential blocks, and Tudor terrace houses. Thames Town is a popular tourist destination, especially for the brides and grooms who pose in front of the picturesque backdrop for their wedding photos. At the same time, the community is also a stagnant ghost town, with most of its units sitting vacant, having been purchased as investments by speculators. The paradoxes and ambiguities of Thames Town typify China's transition into a market economy and the role Shanghai plays within it.

Over the last three decades, Shanghai has become a major globalizing city. A familiar narrative tells us that in 1992 Deng Xiaoping chose Shanghai to become the symbol of the Chinese rebirth following the events of Tiananmen Square. More than a century earlier, the Treaty of Nanking (1842) had transformed what had once been a fishing village into an important international trading port. The domestic and international prestige of colonial Shanghai was long gone when China began to open to the world in the early 1980s. We know that in post-1949 China urban fabrics mirrored logics of uniformity and classlessness and that monumentality of space was only conceded in association with political propaganda (Lin 2007). In accordance with this homogenizing tendency, the government erased the cosmopolitan and bourgeois allure of Shanghai. After forty years of heavy industrialization, only a complete renewal could give the city back its precommunist role as a leading metropolis. Three politicians—Deng Xiaoping on the national level and Shanghai's mayors Jiang Zemin and Zhu Rongji on the local—personified the state's desire to make Shanghai the cultural and financial center of China's integration into the global economy. Shanghai, the "head of the dragon," would drive domestic growth while competing with other major world cities in the international arena (Chen 2009). Since the mid-1990s, especially, the entrepreneurial state and its local agents advanced an aggressive promotional strategy based on new infrastructures, innovative land-use policies, and the designation of special zones (Wu 2003). Although scholars have debated whether Shanghai qualifies for the status of "global city," there is no doubt that it has played a leading economic and symbolic role in China's postreform ascendancy (Sassen 2009; Wu 2009).

The aesthetization of Shanghai's built environment was and continues to be central to its economic growth. Since the 1990s, national and local authorities have increasingly understood that the branding of Shanghai favors the attraction of capital. The decentralization of urban governance assigned a leading role to local authorities in the control of urban development. In the context of rapid urbanization processes, spatial planning served placemaking strategies and reformulated the image of the city from a manufacturing to a service industry center (Wu 2000).

Buildings, public spaces, and entire districts have become commodities to be produced and consumed. Packaged real estate developments, spatial zoning, and creative industries have, since the early 2000s, given Shanghai a vibrant allure. Following two decades of wholesale demolitions, policy makers realized the political and economic power associated with heritage preservation (Weiler 2016; Zhu 2016). Urban renewal came to involve not only the destruction of historical urban fabrics but also their—often invented—reconstruction. Top-down restoration projects such as the one that transformed Xintiandi, and later some more "democratic" variations such as the preservation of Tianzifang, helped create and sell Shanghai's colonial past (Ren 2010; Zhong and Chen 2017; Wang 2011). When nostalgia cannot be "preserved," developers manufacture it from scratch. The outskirts of Shanghai are full of residential developments that imitate historical urban fabrics. Usually—but not exclusively—themed after famous Western places such as Santa Barbara or Notting Hill, these clusters provide the rising middle class with an exclusive, cosmopolitan city (Den Hartog 2010; Li and Zhang 2008; Wu 2010).

The One City, Nine Towns city plan (2001–2005) symbolized Shanghai's new role in the domestic and international arena. To decongest the city center, the municipal government decided to pursue a polycentric growth model. In contrast to the outward industrial expansions of most Chinese cities, Shanghai's new peripheral towns were conceived as residential districts. One city—Songjiang—and nine new smaller urban centers would accommodate seven million inhabitants by 2020 (Figure 15).[1] The design of the urban form was paramount for attracting new residents to the peripheries. Shanghai's mayor Zhu Rongji explicitly asked for each new town to include an area themed after an exotic region. This, he said, would deviate from "the monotonous model of rural town construction" and "build a new order and identity" (Xue and Zhou 2007, 22).

According to the Announcement of the Promotion of Urbanization in Experimental Towns issued by the Shanghai municipality in 2001, the new plan would attract residents by providing them with an "enjoyable natural environment, distinctive townscapes, and modern way of living" (Shen and Wu 2011, 265). As a result, some new towns were themed after European regions such as Italy, Spain, and Germany; others presented an idealized version of Chinese traditional architecture (Chen et al. 2009; Wang et al. 2010).[2]

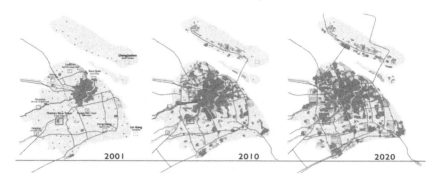

Figure 15. The growth of Shanghai as dictated by the Shanghai One City, Nine Towns plan.

Consistent with the decentralization typical of China's reforms, the Shanghai municipal government provided each district with financial support and let them design the master plans and develop the new towns themselves. Songjiang New Town was the flagship of the plan, given its historical symbolism and ideal location. Originally developed during the Tang Dynasty (seventh to tenth centuries), Songjiang flourished as a textile industry capital during the Ming Dynasty (fourteenth to seventeenth centuries) and declined when Shanghai took over its role after the Opium Wars. In 1958, Songjiang was incorporated into Shanghai's municipality and designated an industrial pole. After an initial period of stagnation, the industrial sector took off in the 1980s—without, however, leading to consistent growth: The urbanization of Songjiang remained lethargic. Even by 2001, more than 60 percent of its population was still employed in the agricultural sector. According to the One City, Nine Towns plan, Songjiang was to become a model of livability, complete with a central business district, university town, historic preserved/reconstructed downtown, beautiful natural landscapes, and the British-style urban design of Thames Town.

Songjiang district's entrepreneurial strategy was to increase land and property values by attracting new residents. To do so, it was necessary to transform Songjiang into a desirable living destination. As did other districts involved in the One City, Nine Towns plan, Songjiang brought in foreign firms in the hopes of giving the city a distinctive allure. In 2000, five international firms were invited to design the new town: three from the United Kingdom, one from Italy, and one from France. The jury was composed of local authorities and urban planning experts from Shanghai's Tongji University. The competitors were asked to work at three different scales, proposing a strategic plan for the whole 60 km² (23.2 mi²) of Songjiang town, a master plan for the 23 km² (8.9 mi²) pilot area, and urban design plans for the 6 km² (2.3 mi²) central business district, the 1 km² (0.38 mi²) transportation hub, and the English-styled Thames Town of the same size (Figures 16 and 17).

The British firm Atkins won the competition in 2001 (Rice 2012). The plan was carried out by the local district in partnership with the municipal government. Construction began in August 2001, and by 2005 the urbanization of the pilot area (north of downtown) was complete. Metro line no. 9, which opened between 2007 and 2008, connected Songjiang to Shanghai, and this immediately increased property values even further than the development project already had. The connection to the city hastened the arrival of new residents. Songjiang district registered the fastest population

1_ Sonhjiang Old Town   2_ Industrial Area   3_ New Residential Development   4_ University Town   5_ Thames Town

Figure 16. The growth of Songjiang New Town as dictated by the Shanghai One City, Nine Towns plan.

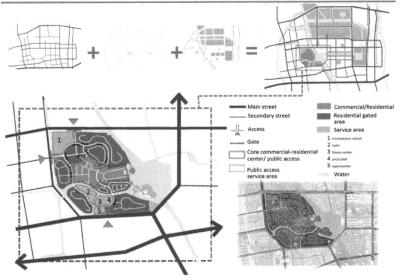

Figure 17. Scheme of Songjiang New Town and Thames Town's developments.

growth of any district between 2000 and 2010. Its population increased by 146.8 percent and counted 1,582,389 residents (Shen 2011; Shen & Wu 2011).[3]

Filling a single square kilometer, Thames Town was planned for 1,100 households (10,000 residents) within the larger 7.36 km² area developed by the Songjiang New Town Development Company (SNTDC), a joint corporation involving the district government and three development companies affiliated with the municipal government. Its British-style architecture makes it the crown jewel of the landscaped environments and green spaces designed to publicize Songjiang as a modern garden city. Completed in different phases (2004/2005 and 2006), the village is enclosed within an artificial lake and canals that SNTDC constructed between 2003 and 2004.

After the land acquisition, master planning, and main infrastructures had been completed, SNTDC leased out land tracts to four private developers. Leaving all the residential areas to the developers but one, SNTDC built some of the public buildings, such as the Songjiang Art Gallery, Songjiang Urban Planning Exhibition Center, sport center, and supermarket. When Thames Town was completed, all the properties sold very quickly, for prices reaching central Shanghai levels. Yet the true value of Thames Town lies in its symbolic power, not in the actual financial rewards that derived from its construction. SNTDC has received far less money from land leasing and property sales than the amount of capital the company invested. SNTDC nonetheless considers Thames Town a success because of the increase of property values that it generated on site as well as in the surrounding areas (Henriot and Minost 2017; Shen 2011).[4]

Thames Town was conceived to be simultaneously a residential community, a tourist destination, and a business center. The free-access compact downtown is surrounded by six, less dense gated communities: Hampton Garden, Rowland Heights, Nottingham Garden, Leeds Garden, Windsor Island, and Kensington Garden—the last being the only gated area with terrace houses instead of single villas. Mostly a pedestrian area, the downtown includes retail and office spaces along with residential five-to-six-store housing blocks—Victoria, Chelsea Garden, and Robin Apartments. Three major public spaces are located on the east-west axis: Love Square, with its Gothic-style church; the monumental semicircular Municipal Square; and the planetarium island, with a marina that overlooks Huating Lake. Smaller open spaces complete with urban furniture are located on the north-south axis.

The residential compounds feature a variety of templates. During fieldwork, I found that the villas of the gated areas vary between 300 and 600 m² (3,230/6,458 ft²); the five-to-six story condos and terraced houses include units ranging from 60 to 260 m² (646/2,799 ft²) in size. The public facilities in Thames Town include public exhibition centers, an international secondary school, a hotel, a fitness center, a supermarket, a kindergarten, and a "foreign-related" office area that welcomes international firms (Figure 18). At the beginning of the project, local authorities planned for Thames Town to include a theater, a stadium, and a conference center. During the design phase, however, SNTDC real-

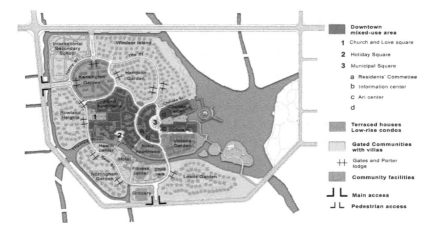

Figure 18. Thames Town's layout, public facilities, and residential areas.

ized that devoting more space to housing would both increase the profits and preserve the village's suburban image (Li 2015).

New developments are usually organized on a regular grid that minimizes construction costs. Thames Town, in contrast, lies across a curved street layout, as if its evolution had followed the natural topography of the site. When some developers protested over the additional expenses associated with the tortuous streets, the Atkins architects designed an underground layout that reduced the construction costs for the electric and water systems while preserving the convoluted streets on the surface (Rice 2012). The eclectic urban form imitates the natural stratification of an old town. Various styles coexist, each evoking a different era and hosting diverse functions.

The western part of Thames Town is the most popular tourist destination. The church approximates the facades, Cosmatesque floors, and glass walls of the neo-Gothic Christ Church of Clifton Town, in Bristol (Figure 19). The church's picturesque Victorian- and Tudor-like surroundings include housing, retail, and restaurants. Moving south, the red and gray brick buildings, which are distributed around the canals and host retail and office spaces, resemble a nineteenth-century industrial town. The contemporary Municipal Square at the center of Thames Town is where the exhibition centers and most offices are located. Heading east

Figure 19. Couple posing in front of the Gothic-like church.

Figure 20. In Thames Town's downtown, Tudor- and Victorian-style buildings imitate the natural stratification of a historical built environment.

from there, a boulevard-like axis leads to the lake. Starting from the planetarium, a southbound path leads into the garden islands, which are adorned with Chinese pavilions, sculptures, and two tearooms (Figure 20).

Elements throughout the village emphasize the Britishness of the development. The custodians wear a red uniform reminiscent of London Beefeaters. Red phone boxes occupy strategic spots in the main public spaces. Deer sculptures greet visitors at the main community entrance on Wencheng Road. Bronze statues of famous Britons—Winston Churchill, Princess Diana, Harry Potter, James Bond, William Shakespeare—are scattered around the streets, the English names of which are also evocative—Oxford Street, Victoria Street, Thames River Walk. Thames Town's commercial activities reinforce the Western-themed atmosphere. The shop in front of the church sells Catholic merchandise such as rosaries, crucifixes, and images of the pope. Although these items are Catholic (and England is overwhelmingly Protestant), their symbolism conveys a general idea of Christianity that the users of Thames town associate with Europe (Figure 21). Art galleries exhibit copies of Western masterpieces and generic European landscapes. At the time of my fieldwork, some Western brands had franchise stores

Figure 21. Interior of downtown Thames Town's church. The Catholic items are sold in a shop in front of the church.

Figure 22. A common green area among the villas within one of the gated residential compounds.

Figure 23. An English-like path winds between the villas inside one of the residential compounds.

in Thames Town, including Lego and Baskin-Robbins. Other English-named shops are owned by Chinese entrepreneurs, who brand their business in accordance with the "Westernness" of the village. This is especially the case with the wedding salons, which represent the most flourishing industry in town.

Thames Town is at once an enormous success and an evident failure. Its spectacular appearance makes it a popular destination for visitors. The British village is a particularly famous stage set for the wedding photography business. Dozens of future brides and grooms crowd the iconic landscapes to pose in front of the town's picturesque backdrops. Local wedding salons offer extensive packages, including costumes, makeup artists, and photographers. At the same time, however, the village has also been given the epithet of "ghost town" in recognition of the fact that most residential units remain vacant: Their owners bought them as an investment and have never lived there.

CHINESE MIMICRY IN URBAN DESIGN:
URBANIZATION AS ACCUMULATION

China's pace and rate of urbanization have drawn enormous attention over the last three decades. Chinese transplanted cityscapes like Thames Town materialize what Fulong Wu (2009) refers to as *urbanization as accumulation.* Chinese cities grow diverse because they host different groups of people—migrant workers, middle classes, nouveaux riches, and the like. Western-styled gated communities respond to the upper middle class's desire to separate itself from the rest of the city. The distinctive urban form of these clusters mirrors the aspirations of its dwellers and ensures high profits for developers. Together with other creative projects and signature architectures, the Western-themed urbanisms give cities iconic landscapes. These landscapes are instrumental to the accumulation of further capital. Themed clusters add an element of prestige, attracting buyers to the new Chinese suburbs. Additionally, tax benefits make the production of transplanted landscapes highly profitable for developers. Urbanization thus coincides with capital accumulation, with theming as a key to the development of new economies. Exploring this phenomenon, Bianca Bosker has coined the term *simulacrascapes* for the ensembles of buildings whose aesthetic reference transcends the Chinese sociocultural context and evokes (stereo)typical Western lifestyles. As I explain below, the success of simulacrascapes speaks to both a cultural attitude toward copying and the specific contradictions of China's market transition.

In the Chinese context, a copy can be as valuable as its original. The distinction between *fake* and *authentic* is not as sharp as in the West, where critics tend to grant a privileged moral value to *original* artifacts. Chinese artists and intellectuals have long understood copying as a culturally legitimized operation. Critics have argued that *the art of making copies* is somehow constitutive of Chinese culture (Fong 1962). The perceived fluidity between the copy and its authentic reference mirrors the traditional Chinese view of existence that sees no distinction between origin and conclusion (Hay 1983). Mandarin has two words for "copy": *fǎgzhi pǐn* and *fùzhi pǐn*, indicating a lower and a higher quality of replication, respectively. Alexander Stille (2002) suggests that this lexicological nuance mirrors the Chinese ambivalence toward copying. Although a copy is initially considered less valuable than its initial model, if a replica captures the essence of the original it then becomes appreciated just as much as its authentic model. The life force that is initially possessed by the authentic source percolates to the copy and makes it a perfect substitute for the original. This dynamic relationship between *real* and *fake* explains why Chinese audiences are less skeptical toward copies than Western commenters tend to be. Still, the recent success of simulacrascapes should be specifically understood in the context of China's transition to a market economy.

The traditional predilection for copying acquired new significance in postreform China. The manufacture of counterfeit merchandise has at once created and gratified the aspirations of the rising Chinese middle class, especially since the 1990s. China is known for the production and distribution of fake products. The term shānzhài (literally, mountain fortress) refers to the practice of reproducing—and at times improving—all sorts of goods. So, in Shenzhen, for example, thousands of painters in the Dafen art village forge famous masterpieces and customize their copies according to their clients' requests. The quality and price of the work are so competitive that the paintings produced in Dafen amount to some 60 percent of artistic reproductions worldwide (Wong 2013). Although shānzhài originally suggested a cheap and inferior copy, the term now glorifies the achievements of Chinese entrepreneurs whose creativity meets the demands of that ever-growing market (Kloet and Scheen 2013; Tse et al. 2009). The new Chinese coffee culture is another case in point. After Starbucks entered China in 1999, coffee houses mushroomed throughout the country, offering beverages sometimes closer to local tastes than the original American products (Henningsen 2012).

Buildings and entire towns are also caught in the shānzhài fever. In 2012, the three towers designed by the architect Zaha Hadid for Wangjing SOHO were cloned and built at a faster pace in Chongqing. A year earlier, the residents of the UNESCO-listed town of Hallstatt, Austria, found out that their village had been entirely replicated in Luoyang, Boluo county. Le Corbusier's masterpiece Ronchamp Chapel was replicated in Zhengzhou in 1994 and demolished in 2000 following the intervention of the Fondation Le Corbusier (Holden-Platt 2012). These episodes are not surprising when we consider how popular reconstructions of historic urban fabrics have recently become.

Traditionally, heritage preservation did not occupy an important role in Chinese culture. The Belgian-Australian sinologist Pierre Ryckmans (2008) has observed that the past was at once spiritually conserved and physically eliminated in Chinese cities. The intangible preservation of traditions—the "cultivation of the moral and spiritual values of the Ancients"—was paradoxically associated with a "curious neglect or indifference . . . towards the material heritage of the past" (1). This traditional approach toward built heritage has recently changed. Since 1982, when the Law on the Protection of Cultural Relics was adopted nationally, the government's attention to preservation has grown exponentially. Aware of both the economic and symbolic implications of the heritage industry, policy makers, developers, and practitioners promote the restoration—which often coincides with the complete reconstruction—of historic buildings.

Preservationists have taken up the task of "restoring the old as it was" (xiūjiù rújiù). The notion of authenticity that corresponds to such a task has little to do with the original materiality of heritage. Conversations on what authenticity means in the Chinese context and on how to mediate between Europe-centered restoration theories and indigenous customs have engaged Chinese scholars since the 1960s. Preservationists translate the word authenticity with two terms: yuán zhēnxìng and zhēnshí xìng—where yuán approximates "original" and zhēn approximates "real." Scholars who use the first term emphasize the need to safeguard the building in "its original state," while those who use the second also acknowledge the importance of making visible the change that a building has undergone through time (Zhu 2016). De facto preservation practices in China rely heavily on the ex-novo construction of buildings that copy—more or less accurately—ancient structures. The Qufu Declaration, a set of restoration guidelines elaborated in 2005, permits rebuilding as long as it is executed with "original" techniques, procedures, and materials. In practice, however, entire villages are built from scratch, giving form to "an idea or an (imagined) past" (Weiler 2016, 222). As scholars have increasingly argued, the newness of the (re)constructed heritage does not impede practitioners or visitors from appreciating its "authenticity" or "historicity" (Ryckmans 2008; Weiler 2016; Zhu 2016).

If copying ancient structures has recently become a common practice, one should note that the replication of alien architectural styles started long before the post-Maoist era. Zou Denong (2001, in Xue 2006) argues that China's exchanges with the West have functioned as three tidal waves, each of which affected architectural production in China. Interpreting the current production of simulacrascapes as a continuation of the traditional philosophy of the copy, Jerome Silbergeld (2013) argues that thematic appropriations date back as far as the third century BCE, when the First

Emperor ordered copies of six palaces that he had conquered to be placed in the new capital city Xianyang. Stylistic mimicry conveyed systems of values and power relations for many centuries.

The use and adaptation of Western forms during the colonial period illustrates this point. Chinese architects replicated the styles of their colonizers but added indigenous elements and adjusted the designs to local climatic conditions (Denison 2017). The adoption of foreign architecture in prereform China culminated with the appropriation of the Soviet modern style. Chairman Mao believed that the exchange between Chinese and Soviet designers would help architects convey socialist content in a typically Chinese national form (Xue 2006, 6). Today, the appropriation of foreign styles is less ideologically driven, but its purposes remain political.

Before spreading into the residential realm, replicas of Western and Chinese buildings were popular attractions in Chinese theme parks. Styled playgrounds had been common in colonial China. Shanghai's Great World Park, which was open from 1916 to 1949, featured a three-dimensional model of the city, among other attractions (Wakeman 1995). Closed during the Maoist period, theme parks reappeared after the economic reforms of 1978. The first amusement park in reform-era China opened in Guangzhou in 1984. Five years later, Shenzhen's Splendid China theme park boasted miniaturized national landmarks that portrayed the country's historical grandiosity and natural beauty. Representing the nation as a "total concept" and a "timeless essence," the compact park emphasized the country's surveyability while also representing China "as a whole" to be admired and consumed at once (Anagost 1993, 586). Other parks themed after popular television series or exotic locales proliferated nationwide throughout the 1990s. In Zhengding, Hebei province, the Journey to the West Palace became so popular that it was replicated in more than fifty locations. Despite their immediate success, however, most theme parks built during the first phase of China's market transition did not remain in business for long. Bad construction quality and fierce competition made it difficult for a theme park to survive more than four years (Liu 2011).

Today, theming strategies help Chinese cities and regions compete with one another by creating iconic urban landscapes that attract capital investment. The marketed symbolism of themed settings offers the rising middle class new consumption opportunities and ensures the success of real estate developments. Theme parks boost tourism, attract capital, and stimulate urbanization. Since the early 2000s especially, economic growth associated with urbanization processes, the increase in consumer leisure time (notably through Golden Weeks and two-day weekends), and a growing number of domestic and international investors have incentivized the development of large entertainment complexes (Campanella 2008; Li and Yang 2007). Compared to their predecessors in the 1990s, developers have grown attentive to parks' location, competition with others, and the maintenance of the attractions. In addition, the themes of the new parks do not necessarily have Western references. In 2009, the Cultural Industry Promotion Plan encouraged the construction of new theme parks with Chinese cultural references (Shien et al. 2014).

Political authorities and investors have increasingly treated tourism and real estate as interdependent aspects of capital attraction (Wu and Xu 2010). The construction of theme parks adds value to the land and boosts the urbanization of their surroundings. For this reason, especially over the last decade, themed parks have been developed within larger real estate complexes that include retail and residential space. The association of themed parks and residential design models guarantees developers rapid profits and ensures that local governments increase land values (Lu et al. 2011; Zhang and Shan 2016). During this time, the boundaries between theme parks and residential clusters have become increasingly blurred. Developers transplant Western-like cityscapes into new residential clusters and attract new consumers to the suburbs (Wu 2006). Themed residential clusters have proliferated throughout China, gratifying the fantasies and aspirations of the new middle class. Land and housing reforms have proven essential to the commodification of space.

As is well known, the construction boom that followed the end of the dānwèi system raised living standards and created stratified housing groups. Some "got rich" before others did, as Deng Xiaoping had prophesized in his 1979 plan for a prosperous society—xiǎokāng shèhuì (Hewitt 2007). Since the early 1990s, urban professionals and skilled employees in the public and private sectors acquired wealth. These salaried populations formed a large group of new consumers along with the entrepreneurial elites that had begun accumulating capital (Tomba 2004). Home ownership became a status symbol through which middle-to-high-income buyers could express their newly acquired prosperity (Davis 2000; Z. Li 2010; Man 2011). Western-style residential communities grew popular among the upwardly mobile middle class. Iconic, symbolic, and extravagant urban forms continue to characterize new residential clusters and contribute to the mythicization of a private "oasificated" domestic life (Fraser 2000).

Transplanted cityscapes add a level of prestige and help market the new suburbs. Over the last three decades, China has shifted from a monocentric to a polycentric system of organization. This change was initially enabled by the land-leasing reforms that pushed local governments to embark in vast capital-attracting developments (Chen et al. 2009). Changes in consumer preferences further enhanced the success of exurban expansion. Particularly since the 2000s, suburban clusters have become the favored living destination of the nouveaux riche. Jie Shen and Fulong Wu (2013) recognize three factors that caused this shift in residential preferences: the relaxation of systems of control over urban populations and the end of welfare housing allocations; the rise of consumer culture; and the fact that suburban developments were built to represent a greener, privacy-oriented, and exclusive alternative to the city center. The new suburban imaginary determined the success of the residential enclaves. This imaginary is intertwined with the symbolism of the gates and walls of the communities. Chinese residential communities have always featured walls. The traditional walled compounds remained separate from the city while housing diverse groups of people. Contemporary gated communities, in contrast, target a homogeneous clientele in search of exclusivity, civilization, and social homogeneity (Pow 2009; Wu 2005, 2010).

Western architectural features are essential for branding the new "golden ghettoes" (Giroir 2006). In 2003, the Beijing-based Horizon Research Consultancy Group, a market research firm, found that 70 percent of developers considered Western styles a profitable marketing tool (Rosenthal 2003). This proportion still seems accurate today, given that customized versions of Santa Barbara, Versailles, and the like continue to pop up throughout the country (Shepard 2016).

Themed residential enclaves are usually relatively quick to put together. An assembly-line-like design process ensures that the final product is delivered on time and that the buildings' proportions resemble their Western references. I participated in the design of three European-type residential communities when I worked as an architect in a Shanghai design firm in 2012. My boss believed that my Caucasian appearance would benefit the firm because it would convince the clients—mostly developers from outside Shanghai—that what we had designed was "real." For this reason, I was invited to participate in numerous meetings regardless of whether I had been directly involved in the business at hand.

Both the interaction with the clients and the design process followed a rigid script. The architects' team would show the client various renderings (computer-generated images created with three-dimensional models), each evoking a different atmosphere. The design firm I worked for usually offered clients a choice of ten atmospheres, of which six were labeled as "traditional Western," two as "traditional Chinese," and two as "modern." Each rendering came with a series of evocative images of real places that had inspired that particular design style—a picture of St. Peter's Square in Rome, for example, would evoke a "classic" atmosphere, while an image of the Quartier Latin in Paris recalled a "romantic" ambience.

Once the clients picked their preference, the designers would turn their attention to a technical catalogue of features that corresponded to that particular atmosphere. The catalogue contains instructions on how to maintain the right proportions of the facades and floor plans. It also includes variations on architectural elements, such as diverse capitals and columns, that the designer chooses when assembling the final building (Figures 24 and 25). Designing a luxury gated community of twenty-five villas takes a group of four architects approximately one month. The American-educated architect-in-chief I worked with told me that before the "catalogue method" it took the designers four months to draw the same plans and facades. He also told me that about 80 percent of their clients chose one of the traditional Western atmospheres.

The designers use various stratagems to preserve the Western appearance while making the gated community comfortable to live in for their Chinese clientele. The intimate scale of the European city is usually widened in these simulacrascapes. This happens, for example, when an iconic place such as the Piazza San Marco in Hangzhou is made bigger than its original reference (Bosker 2013). Streets are usually wider and more comfortable to drive on

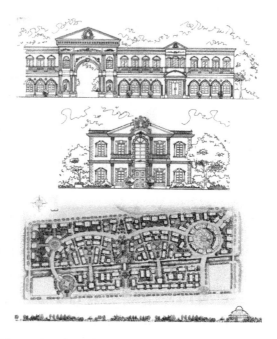

Figure 24. Examples of "Italian" neighborhood and facades designed by the author for a development company in Shanghai.

Figure 25. Examples of "Italian" facades designed by the author for a development company in Shanghai.

than their European counterparts. The single villas are detached from the perimeter of the lot as in the Western fashion, but the floor plans are often adapted according to Chinese customs—for example, the distribution of the room follows the rules of *fēngshuǐ*, and kitchens are designed in accordance with local cooking habits. The residents are free to decorate the interiors as they please, and they enjoy this liberty. But all residents consent to a strict system of rules to make sure that the outdoor spaces remain in conformity with the theme and that the overall atmosphere stays "authentic." These rules are negotiated within the community and can change through time depending on the residents' ideas and necessities. The names of the gated communities are carefully chosen to help cultivate an exotic allure. Developers choose evocative Western names that their clienteles must both find appealing and be able to remember easily. A developer of a French-style community once asked me to find a name that sounds European enough but that his Mandarin-speaking clients could still easily pronounce.

Transplanted cityscapes typify the intricate relationship between globalization, urbanization, and capital attraction in China. Theming strategies have profoundly affected the new Chinese landscapes of consumption from both a physical and sociocultural standpoint. If homeownership is a status symbol for the new middle class, transplanted cityscapes further please these new consumers by offering them iconic, symbolic, and "oasificated" places to live. While developers and local governments encourage the production of simulacrascapes, the success of these themed residential enclaves is equally determined by the choice of their residents. Themed residential clusters elicit derisive reactions from most Western observers in spite of their popular success—or perhaps because of it.

BEYOND "KITSCH" AND "FAKE"

Scholars from both outside and within China have looked with interest at the success of simulacrascapes. A Google search for "copycat architecture China" shows that simulacrascapes continue to stimulate the curiosity of major Western newspapers and TV stations. Most observers, however, tend to ridicule the Chinese imitations by associating them with the greediness of developers, the lack of creativity on the part of designers, and the bad taste of consumers. Most articles on Chinese simulacrascapes label them as fake, kitsch, or bizarre. These articles contain images that emphasize the comic *exoticness* of simulacrascapes: The copied iconic building usually stands in the background, contrasted against the figures of residents or construction workers in front. The *Chineseness* of the people in the picture is typically emphasized through stereotypical elements such as bicycles and motorbikes overloaded with people or goods, bamboo construction barrels, or Mandarin characters on signage. These elements stimulate the curiosity of Western observers and stress the irony of the themed landscapes.

Chinese developers might essentialize exotic forms to construct a sense of otherness for profit. Yet the Western journalists who criticize them do the same. Academics also treat the Chinese pre-dilection for simulacrascapes as a superficial and cheap act of imitation (Hassenpflug 2008). Other commenters have gone be-yond the folkloristic aspects of simulacrascapes to explore their sociocultural and economic implications. These observers broad-ly agree that the transplantation of cityscapes symbolizes nei-ther the uncritical appropriation of Western forms nor the loss of an "authentic" Chinese identity. Bianca Bosker (2013) wrote the first book entirely dedicated to the Chinese fascination for architectural mimicry. Her thorough analysis reveals important aspects of simulacrascapes in contemporary China. Bosker argues that the "faux" landscapes inspired by Western built forms are in fact "original copies." Rescaled, adapted, and adjusted to local needs, these clusters simply continue the old Chinese tradition of copying the alien at a new scale and pace. Bosker's interviews with developers and designers reveal that, beyond the greed for profit, these professionals are proud not only to reproduce but to improve Western architectures. For them, the appropriation of foreign styles is itself a status symbol. Bosker reminds us that simulacrascapes—their origin and success or failure—portray the aspirations, hopes, and struggles of their residents and creators and cannot be superficially dismissed as mere copies.

Thomas Campanella (2008) reiterates this point by offering a rich narrative of the relationship between theming and the Chi-nese "urbanisms of ambition." There is no doubt that themed resi-dential clusters represent far more than dwellings. In choosing their preferred theme, homebuyers are consciously picking and buying an identity and lifestyle. Transplanted geographies are not the only option that developers use to brand properties; sustain-able or smart are equally powerful labels. The "manic eclecticism" (Campanella 2008, 207) of the themed residential cluster should not distract us from understanding the cultural significance of theming in the Chinese context. Transplanted cityscapes are "postmodern spaces of consumption" constructed for the delight of the new "immense middle class" (242). Campanella argues that the reason why themed settings are so successful is because they enable Chinese consumers to overcome the "denial of history" that prevailed during the Maoist era. That is, the settings that imitate historical urban fabrics help Chinese people to reappropriate the past, even if that past is geographically remote.

Looking at the Shanghai New Towns built in accordance with the One City, Nine Towns city plan, Harry Den Hartog (2010) emphasizes how these spaces present a mix of Western and Chinese features. The Western style allows the rising middle class to escape the modern Chinese city's threat of anonymity. However, the affluent residents of the luxury compounds also remain profoundly tied to their Chinese customs. Chinese interior décor and a southern orientation allow these residents to feel "at home."

Chinese architects and developers do not appropriate Western styles uncritically. Planning concepts, techniques, and ideas inevitably circulate among regions and influence how people and professionals change space. Traditional conversations on how architectural prototypes travel among places reinforce the rhetorical distinction between origin and destination. Looking at former colonies, in the past critics adopted a linear narrative of progress through which cultures of planning spread from "more advanced" to "less developed" regions. But knowledge transfer is never unidirectional. Increasingly aware of the circular relationships that fabricate local identities, scholars have recently shed light on the context-dependent forces that translate imported ideas into indigenized urban forms. Power relations at different scales, grassroots movements, and the quotidian negotiations of multiple actors affect the transfer process (Haley and Upton 2010; Olds 2004). As is the case for other rapidly urbanizing regions, the origin/destination narrative proves inadequate for interpreting the Chinese appropriation of Western architectures.

China's transition to a market system has challenged local designers with new questions. Professionals experience a condition of permanent uncertainty that arises when the top-down mechanisms enabled by the Chinese state confront the unpredictable power dynamics of each development at the local level. At the same time, the exchange of ideas and collaboration between local and foreign professionals push Chinese architects to ponder issues of form and identity. In these circumstances of uncertainty and new cultural exchanges, Chinese architects have increasingly questioned their positionality. Foreign architectures have influenced contemporary design practices since China's opening in 1978. Western influences initially infiltrated China from other Asian regions such as Hong Kong, Taiwan, and Singapore. When the media disseminated images of Europe and America during the 1980s, most Chinese came to see anything Western as inherently superior. Western planning and architectural theories became accessible to Chinese audiences through translations of the works of scholars such as Kevin Lynch, Robert Venturi, and Christopher Alexander. In the 1990s, local governments started inviting Western firms to design public buildings. This is still a practice today in nearly every mid-to-high-ranking city. As Western architectures appeared all over the country, however, Chinese architects began to question the idea that the "foreign is always superior" (Xue 2006, 47). Today, this doubt productively lies at the core of Chinese architectural debates.

Confronted with the paradoxes and ambiguities of ever-changing political scenarios, Chinese professionals must negotiate between their ideals and the political and cultural contexts in which they operate. Theming is one of the techniques that Chinese architects employ to cope with the uncertainties they face. Since the early 2000s, designers have debated the necessity of reconsidering the specificities of local contexts and honoring the country's own rich heritage. Their communication with foreign professionals enables a two-way exchange that influences architectural theories and practices in China and abroad. In search of an autonomous architectural language—yet one tied to new global dynamics—Chinese designers have elaborated tactics to express their creativity in transcending mainstream design conventions (Santi 2017; Yung 2006; Zhu 2005). The collective ambitions, desires, and inventions of China's transition materialize in what Li (2006) has identified as the "five points of the new Chinese architecture": novelty, monumentality, bigness, swiftness, and cheapness. The adoption of Western forms satisfies these points and suits the Chinese penchant for pragmatism. Despite their contentious symbolism, themed landscapes facilitate economic growth and respond promptly to the demand for housing (Ren 2010).

Not all of the designers of simulacrascapes endorse the aesthetic codes or the political circumstances behind the spread of themed settlements. For example, when the Shanghai-based architect Ma Qingyun designed a fake antique pavilion for the Qu Shui Yuan Park in Qingpu, he augmented the copy with a decontextualized ultramodern canopy. Standing in sharp contrast to the rest of the project, the canopy subtly declares the *fakeness* of the traditional-looking surroundings and enacts a form of resistance toward the proliferation of simulacrascapes. We must also note that the revenues that come from the design of themed residential clusters enable architects to experiment on other projects. For example, most designers that I talked with divide their work between Western-style developments and small-scale independent projects. Themed settings might not result from thoughtful invention, but their production gives designers the financial security to be creative elsewhere.

Considering the uncertainties that Chinese architects are confronted with, Li Xiangning argues that these designers navigate the status quo through a "Make-the-Most-of-It" approach: They find subtle ways to concretize their aspirations within the ever-evolving and ambiguous Chinese political context. In Li's view, "Make-the-Most-of-It architecture might not be the best, but it definitely suits China the best" (X. Li 2008, 233). Criticizing the derision of Western-like urban replicas made by most observers, scholars have also emphasized that simulacrascapes do not deceive their audiences. On the contrary, they manifest themselves as "a kind of real-fakery." Chinese themed clusters "frankly" tell the story of their imitation of the West, allowing for users' "honest" negotiations of meanings. Thanks to their candor, these spaces become naturalized within their surroundings over time (X. Li 2010, 236). More importantly, the presence of foreign urban forms modifies local identities.

The landscapes of "fake" take on a degree of originality through the social production of space. The users of Western-style clusters resignify imported typologies and symbols. Tim Oakes (2006) insists that the European-centered association of authenticity with the material originality of artifacts has little significance in the Chinese context. In his thorough analysis of ethnic-themed tourist villages, Oakes encourages us to consider how notions of "real" and "fake" are continuously negotiated and constructed in the context of China's modernization. The success of Chinese theme parks, then, does not indicate an "unreflexive loss of authenticity." Rather, Oakes argues the theme park is an *authentic replica*" in which the notion of authenticity is exploited "to both mark the originality of tradition and the replicability of modernity" (169). As newly built historic buildings, simulacrascapes also become authentic through the everyday appropriations and negotiations of their users. The Victorian facades, Versailles-like gates, and pseudo-Venetian canals acquire diverse meanings depending on who is using them. The spaces of simulacra become unique stages "where globalized references and local customs coexist" (Henriot and Minost 2017, 86). The everyday activities that take place on these stages concoct an original "civilization mix" that makes the themed residential clusters unique (Giroir 2006).

Thus far, I have argued that we should not pigeonhole simulacrascapes as the result of an uncritical appropriation of Western styles. Nor we can label the transplanted cityscapes as inauthentic copies. Rather, we should consider that the diffusion and success of simulacrascapes reveal the specific nuances and contradictions of China's transition. I draw upon these considerations to suggest that exploring how diverse groups use and signify the styles adopted for residential settings can unveil the social and political implications of theming. As I will show in the next chapter, Thames Town is an ideal site to investigate these dynamics, given its ambivalent status as a popular tourist destination, pleasing residential community, and ghost town.

ENDNOTES

1. Shen and Wu (2012, 190) report that the Shanghai Master Plan system for 2000–2020 comprises four levels: "a central city with a population of 8 million; 11 new suburban cities with a population of 200,000 to 400,000 each; 22 central towns with a population of 50,000 each; and 88 ordinary towns with a population of 20,000 to 30,000 each."

2. According to the 2001 planning document, the new towns would mimic England (Songjiang), Germany (Anting, Jiading district), Italy (Pujiang, Minhang district), traditional southern China (Zhujiajiao, Qingpu

district), the Netherlands (Gaoqiao, Pudong district), Canada (FengJing, Jinshan district), Sweden (Luodian, Baoshan district), Spain (Fencheng, Fengxian district), southern China (Chengjiazhen), and a general European-American West (Zhoupu of Nanhui and Buzhen of Chongming). Lingang and Chenjiazhen were developed from 2004, the former being a separate project directly developed by the municipality.

3. In her dissertation *Suburban Development in Shanghai: A Case of Songjiang*, Shen Jie (2011) provides a rich, thorough, and detailed narrative linking the development of Songjiang within the context of the new Chinese predilection for suburbia.

4. SNTDC cleared a total of 360 million yuan in profits after investing 1.4 billion yuan. Shen Jie (2011, 143–46) provides a detailed description of SNTDC's returns and investments.

CHAPTER 3

Everyday Life in the English Village of Shanghai

QUESTIONS AND METHODS

In approaching Thames Town, I was struck by an enormous contradiction: The iconic public spaces were crowded with people, but the residential areas were empty. On the one hand, Thames Town is an important center of the wedding photography industry. Professional photographers portray dozens of future brides and grooms in a standard sequence of poses—the funny moment, the romantic proposal, the happy ending. With their colorful and matching outfits, these couples have become an attraction themselves—tourists visit Thames Town just to see them. On the other hand, Thames Town maintains the spectral allure of a Potemkin village, housing less than a quarter of the population it was planned for.[1] Occupancy rates remain low because many owners purchased properties as a form of investment, never intending actually to reside there. Many units also remain incomplete, lacking floors, tiles, and doors. The open windows, hanging laundry, and scooters one sporadically sees in the downtown residential areas signal the almost exclusive presence of squatting migrant construction workers who occupy vacant units.

These two seemingly antithetical aspects—the vitality of the touristic spaces and the ghostly emptiness of the residential areas—are, in fact, complementary. I would argue that both qualities indicate that Thames Town's themed design affects the ways people behave in and experience its spaces. Its Western appearance attracts visitors to downtown areas and also fosters a sense of pride among residents. At the same time, the presence of the theme shapes how people exclude those who do not behave or look appropriately. In this section, I investigate these dynamics by looking at the kinds of personal and spatial relationships that emerge in Thames Town as a result of its British theme. Three questions structure my exploration: Why do people choose to be in Thames Town? To whom are these spaces open and desirable, and to whom do they remain unappealing or closed off? When and why do its users follow the Thames Town script, and when do they break from that script?

Observation, survey questionnaires, and interviews allowed me to answer these questions, over two phases. I conducted fieldwork throughout the year I lived in Shanghai between June 2012 and March 2013. I engaged with four groups of users: the tourists, the wedding couples, the residents, and the employees (both the guards and the construction workers who live in Thames Town while they renovate the units). In July 2013 and September 2014, I went back in situ and met with some of the interviewees again. During the first three months of my fieldwork, I drew maps to track how the various groups of users behaved in Thames Town and collected survey data via questionnaire. In the second phase of the investigation, I continued observing and conducting interviews. I spent about three days a week in Thames Town, sleeping in an accommodation outside of the village because I could not afford the hotel within the official boundaries of the community.

Thames Town was accessible only by car: The subway line stopped a few miles from the village, and no buses were available at the time. I took a taxi from the metro stop, but most visitors and employees used their private vehicles to reach Thames Town directly. At the time of my investigation, I only possessed basic conversational Mandarin, so I hired a research assistant, Lian, to help me distribute the questionnaires and translate the interviews.

My whiteness and affiliation with Tongji University were powerful passports that smoothed my way with the residents. Most guards and construction workers were initially less interested in responding my questions, although eventually some of them allowed me to spend time with them.

I began with nonparticipant observation of the downtown public spaces, which allowed me to get acquainted with the area and its user groups. I carried out an observation hourly for about fifteen minutes from 8:00 am to 8:00 pm on both weekdays and weekends. I observed and mapped the pathways and static activities and coded the diverse users with letters: "b" for brides, grooms, and their entourage of photographers and make-up artists; "t" for tourists and residents (which two groups I could not visually distinguish from each other); and "w" for workers, such as the guards and construction workers. Although the population increased during the weekends (the flow picks up around 11:00 am and 4:00 pm), their activities did not vary significantly over the course of the day. The tourists, couples, and workers acted in predictable patterns and tended to occupy the same spaces. The construction workers were the only exceptions because they tended to remain in the areas where they were employed, unless they squatted into the downtown units or went in front of the gated areas to socialize.

The questionnaires I collected helped me understand the sociodemographic characteristics of each user group. My research assistant and I collected a total of 175 questionnaires distributed among the engaged couples (20), the visitors (50), the employees (20, comprising 10 construction workers and 10 guards), and the residents (85, with 30 villa and 50 condo/terraced house inhabitants). Although this is not a statistically significant sample, the respondents' answers assisted me in developing the subsequent steps of the research and acquainted me with some of the people that I interviewed later. We initially relied on convenience sampling, just asking people we met to fill in the questionnaire. These respondents then helped us find others, so that convenience sampling led to chain-referral sampling.

Lian and I approached the tourists and the engaged couples while they were visiting the downtown area. We waited at the gates of the residential communities and asked passersby to fill in the questionnaires. The residents who accepted our requests usually put us in contact with their neighbors. We reached out to the guards while waiting for the residents at the gates. Finally, we approached the construction workers when we saw them sitting outside the units they worked in. As with the residents, most workers introduced us to their colleagues after responding to the questionnaire.

The questionnaires had four sections common to all user groups and contained mostly closed-ended lists and rankings. The first section investigated the respondents' reasons for being in Thames Town. It asked for explanations of why people were there, how they had heard of the village, and how much time they spent there. The second section centered on the appearance of the space and asked respondents about their previous travel experiences and whether Thames Town resembled any place that they had ever seen in person or otherwise—on TV, in photographs, and so on. This section asked people to identify three features that made Thames Town "Chinese" and three that made it "English." I also asked the respondents whether and in what ways had Thames Town matched their expectations in terms of appearance, quality of space, and services offered. The third section investigated how people used the spaces, asking which sites the users had visited in Thames Town, which they liked better and why, and how they liked the other people who were using the space. The questionnaire also asked the respondents to list anything they would have liked to do in the town but did not do and what prevented them from doing it. Finally, the fourth section asked for demographic and personal information, such as age, income, and education. We distributed a second questionnaire tailored for the wedding couples and the residents. The couples were asked for information regarding the photo shoots—why they decided to use Thames Town, how much the photography services cost, which salon they were hiring, and so on. The residents were asked information about their house— whether their furniture was Chinese or Western, whether they had modified anything in the layout after living in the house and why, whether and how they had changed any habits since they had moved to Thames Town, and so on. Most respondents answered all the questions, although some left the demographics section blank.

During the second phase of the investigation, I conducted in-depth interviews with some of the respondents I met during the first phase. I interviewed two engaged couples, three tourists, three employees (two construction workers and one guard), and six residents (four villa owners and two apartment occupants, one renter and one owner). The interviews lasted between ninety and 120 minutes and were held in a location chosen by the respondent. The residents wanted to be interviewed in their own homes and the guards and construction workers in either their workplace or where they were living at that time. I talked with the couples and tourists in the public spaces of downtown Thames Town or in the wedding salons.

The interviews were structured with open-ended queries, interspersed with probing questions. The script included five topical areas: personal history, reasons for using Thames Town, relationship with tourism, awareness of the theme, and—for the residents—a focus on living habits and furnishing choices. Along with the interviews, I also continued to conduct observations, particularly inside the residential communities. By coincidence, this phase of investigation in Thames Town occurred at the same time that I changed professional positions. I was no longer a research fellow at the Heritage Preservation Department at the Tongji Urban Planning Design Institute; I now worked in a mid-tier Shanghai architectural firm, where I got involved in the design of several themed communities.

In the next section, I present the data I collected on the personal and spatial relationships that are emerging in Thames Town. My field investigations revealed that the presence of the theme at once included and excluded the users of the village by creating a specific politics of belonging. On the one hand, the theme became an instrument of cohesion because the tourists, the residents, and the engaged couples willingly modified their habits in order to construct and preserve the British atmosphere. At the same time, the theme also excluded migrant workers, who did not conform to the town's aesthetic and behavioral codes. These circumstances show that the symbolism of the British theme enabled implicit and explicit mechanisms of control. However, the users' quotidian practices also revealed that Thames Town is not a space of absolute control, demonstrating that the village also functions as the stage of provisional appropriations and unexpected significations.

THE USERS AND USES OF THAMES TOWN

One of the most interesting finding that came from my observation and questionnaires is that although various groups coexist in the village, they do not necessarily overlap in space. In fact, each user group is concentrated in a specific part of town (Figure 26). The engaged couples stay in the thematic downtown core. The tourists visit this core but also extend their visit to the green spaces of the island. The residents do not like to mix with the other groups and for this reason tend to remain inside the gated areas. Finally, the guards and construction workers gather at the edges of the residential communities using the porters' lodge—the detached one-room structure built at the entrance of each gated area—as a space of encounter and exchange. While all of the users like the Western appearance of the built environment, the groups interpret and use the Englishness of the village in different ways.

Engaged couples. Most of the future brides and grooms are in their early twenties, have college degrees, and live in the Shanghai metropolitan area—although only half of the respondents were born there. The majority of the couples met in person. Others met online; fewer than half met because a relative arranged the marriage. Most couples visit Thames Town for the first time on the day of their photo shoot and stay there from 9:00 am to 5:00 pm. They heard about the "English" location from their friends or the internet and chose the wedding salon by looking at sample portfolios on the web. All respondents said that Thames Town strongly resembled England, although almost none had ever visited that country.

Their idea of England, some respondents explained, was inspired by TV shows and movies such as Downton Abbey and Harry Pot-

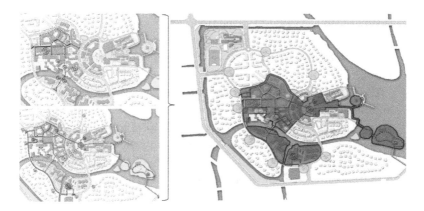

Figure 26. Maps describing the activities of different user groups in the free-access downtown area. At top left, the orange color describes the paths (primary and secondary) and the static activities of the engaged couples. At bottom left, red indicates the tourists' paths and static activities (primary and secondary); yellow indicates the areas outside the gates where the migrant workers meet. At right, while couples and tourists overlap in space in the core downtown area, the migrant workers do not mix with them and stay outside the gates.

ter. The engaged couple usually comes to Thames Town a few months before the actual ceremony. Their photos will be shown to family and friends on the day of the wedding and in some cases distributed as souvenirs. Professional photographers direct the poses of the brides and grooms, and hairdressers and makeup artists change their look according to the style of the picture—the shoots commonly feature between two and six styles, including traditional Chinese, "Modern Western," and "Revolutionary China" (Figure 27). The photo shoot costs between 20 and 50 percent of the total wedding budget and prices vary greatly. In 2013, a first-tier salon like the Milan charged from 2,600 up to 78,000 yuan (300 to 12,000 USD). The photographers match each of the styles the couples choose with a different backdrop: The trees and canals go well with the Chinese themes, the church with the classic Western style, and the Victorian and Tudor streets are perfect for the "Romantic European" pictures. The photographers compete fiercely. Their credibility as photographers of English-style weddings increases if the photographer has previously photographed actual Western models or, even better, if they have worked in Europe.

The more expensive packages include pictures taken outdoors and indoors, in the studios the most prestigious salons own downtown. The cheapest option, at 650 Yuan (100 USD at the time), is to pay a photographer and a hairdresser to style and photograph the bride and groom directly on the streets of Thames Town. The wedding salons are located almost exclusively in the "historic" part of downtown, which is also where the photo shoots normally take place. This perhaps explains why all of the wedding couples listed the church as their favorite landmark in Thames Town and stated that they were not interested in going outside of the thematic core. Interestingly, only a few couples said that they would like to live in Thames Town on a permanent basis. Although most respondents enjoyed experiencing the village on a special occasion, they suspected they might get tired of its atmosphere were they to be in Thames Town every day.

Tourists. Most tourists live in the Songjiang new residential settlements and visit Thames Town in family groups (usually two

Figure 27. Engaged couples wearing different matching outfits: "Western Romantic," "Red Guards," and "Western Classic."

college-educated parents in their thirties with a child under ten). The average tourist drives between twenty and fifty minutes, two weekends a year, to spend three and a half hours in Thames Town. Although the aesthetic appearance of the settlement is an important reason the tourists visit the town, the respondents also indicated that the greenery they find there is equally important. Some visitors come to the village to fish in the canals and to spend a few hours sitting on the grass of the eastern islands. For this reason, the tourists' paths extend beyond the typical itinerary of the engaged couples and stretch over the whole community.

The wedding couples themselves represent an important attraction for the tourists, who take pictures of the brides and grooms and like to comment on their look. As indicated earlier, most respondents have never visited Europe. They identified Thames Town as "English" in particular because of the church, the style of the buildings, and the name of the streets. The tourists indicated both the greenery and the presence of the wedding couples as features that made Thames Town "Chinese." In contrast to the engaged couples, the tourists said that they would like to live in Thames Town, although they understood it was too expensive for them (Figure 28).

Employees. The construction business thrives in Thames Town, as it does everywhere else in China. Both in the downtown area and

Figure 28. Visitors to Thames Town engaging in what they perceive to be English-like activities, such as a trolley-bus trip, a Sunday brunch, and picnics.

in the gated communities, retail and residential spaces undergo continuous renovation. Although I was unable to find official information, the migrant workers I talked to told me that there were about two hundred people employed in the construction business at the time of my investigation. Most of the construction workers had lived in Shanghai for under three years. The majority was in their early thirties and had brought along a child—usually under four—and a partner also employed in the construction business. Other migrants were in their fifties and in most cases had moved to Thames Town alone. I also met some construction workers who had moved with their extended family, in that their group comprised parents, children, and in-laws.

Most of the workers spend about a year in Thames Town, renovating different units in the residential gated communities and the commercial areas. They usually live in the units they are renovating. When they live in the gated areas, they remain inside the houses: The residents do not want them hanging out in their communities and ask the guards to police their presence. Some of these migrant workers choose to squat in vacant units downtown, where they are relatively free to cook, spend time on the streets, and hang their washing outside (Figure 29). In the squatted units, families lived together in one room and usually shared the apartment with one other family. Single migrants instead lived with other three or four workers in one room. Although they live in Thames Town, the workers remain separate from the other residents and form an independent community in which they provide one another with food, entertainment, and childcare.

Although the style of the buildings and the large residential units in Thames Town fascinated the construction workers, most of them said they would not like to live there because it is too expensive and especially because the lack of grocery stores and markets make life uncomfortable. The guards in the gated communities expressed the same sentiment. Exclusively men mostly in their fifties, many of the guards officially live in the new developments of Songjiang New Town. They avoid commuting to their homes on a daily basis, however, and instead often sleep in their lodges or squat in any available empty units they find. The por-

Figure 29. The employees of Thames Town: migrant workers (*L, C*) and a Hampton Garden guard (*R*).

ters' lodges function as a gathering point not only for the guards but also for the migrant workers who reside temporarily in the gated compounds. Often forbidden to spend time outdoors in the residential compounds, the migrants have to go to the gates of the community to enjoy fresh air. Some of the porters' lodges function as little market places where guards informally—and without the residents' knowledge—sell fruits and vegetables to the construction workers, who lack easy means of reaching Songjiang.

Residents. There are three types of residential buildings in Thames Town. The single villas are detached units of two or four floors with five to fifteen rooms that vary between 300 and 600 m² (3,230/6,458 ft²), with a private yard of 100 or 200 m² (1,076 or 2,152 ft²). The terrace houses are contiguous units with private access, two or three floors, an average surface area of 220 m² (2,368 ft²), four to seven rooms, and a private yard of 45 or 80 m² (484 or 861 ft²). The condominium apartments usually extend over one floor (some are duplex), have between one and five rooms, and vary from 55 to 200 m² (538 to 2,368 ft²); some also have a balcony. Two kinds of families are likely to inhabit Thames Town: retired couples in their sixties and young families composed of two adults in their forties—usually holders of advanced degrees—and a child under the age of fifteen.

Before moving, all of the respondents had previously lived in smaller homes usually located in newly developed and high-density areas of Shanghai. Most respondents bought their property between 2004 and 2006, directly from the developers. Only a minority of residents purchased their units from private owners in subsequent years. Shen Jie (2011) reports that, after completion, apartments in Thames Town were sold for 4000 to 6,500 Yuan/m², while the villas went for 6,000 to 9,000 Yuan/m.² These prices have increased steadily in the years since they were first put on the market. By the time of my field investigation, local real estate agencies were listing secondhand apartments for prices ranging between 13,000 and 15,000 Yuan/m², terrace houses for between 16,000 and 18,500 Yuan/m², and villas for between 40,000 and 47,000 Yuan/m². The properties in Thames Town were considerably more expensive than their counterparts in surrounding areas—villa and condo prices were, respectively, twice and 1.3 times the price of their equivalents in Songjiang New Town. About half of the residents relied on mortgages to buy their homes; the other half were able to draw primarily on family savings.

The Western appearance of the built environment, the green spaces and water, the future property values, and the perception of safety were the principal factors that influenced residents to buy properties in Thames Town. Most parents also considered the international school to be a decisive factor. When asked whether Thames Town was more Chinese or English, residents hesitated in their response. To most of them, the Chineseness and Britishness of Thames Town were not discernable and equally important for the identity of the community.

While the church, the streets' layout, and the appearance of the buildings signaled Englishness to respondents, they listed the greenery, the noise, and the people in the village as examples of Chineseness. This perception is one reason the residents tend not to spend time in the downtown public spaces. Although they occasionally take walks through the themed core and the green islands, they believe that the spaces are too crowded and the restaurants overpriced. Other residents, especially those who had traveled or lived abroad, do not like the restaurants in downtown Thames Town because the food they serve is not "authentic" European. Most residents likewise expressed mixed feelings about the wedding businesses. While some respondents did not approve of the wedding photo shoots, seeing them as noisy and dirty, most recognized that the wedding business is a thriving activity that increases the value of Thames Town and promotes the village to the world.

The residents have great autonomy to customize their home interiors after purchasing their unit. Almost one-third of the respondents reported substantially modifying their layouts in order to make their homes better fit their needs or to make them consistent with the Chinese fengshui traditions—to adjust the orientation of the rooms, for example, or to improve ventilation. About two-thirds paid an interior design firm to furnish their houses; the rest chose the materials and styles on their own. Almost all residents bought new furniture when they moved.

Although a quarter of the respondents could not identify the style of their furnishings, the majority declared that they chose their furniture intentionally either to imitate an English house— about three-quarters—or a Chinese one. This was particularly evident in the responses of the villa owners, who emphasized that the British theme of Thames Town was the primary reason they chose to style their interiors in accordance or in contrast with the rest of the settlement. Most villa owners also chose to give their private gardens an English, Chinese, or Japanese look. Sometimes the style of the garden contrasts with the interior, perpetuating the pastiche-like atmosphere of the ensemble (Figure 30).

PARTICIPATING IN AND CONSTRUCTING
THE BRITISH ATMOSPHERE

The presence of the British theme affects the ways people use and understand the spaces of the village. The sharp contrast between Thames Town and the rest of Songjiang New Town is something

Figure 30. Residents of the residential gated communities in their homes.

both visitors and residents appreciate. During the design phase, the Songjiang New Town Development Company asked the Atkins architects to create a totalizing atmosphere while also emphasizing the uniqueness of Thames Town (Rice 2012). The shape and appearance of the built environment clearly differentiates Thames Town from the rest of Songjiang. The Gothic bell tower, the English-language signage, and the guards' Beefeater-style uniforms tell visitors that they are entering a space completely different from its surroundings. Inside the community, the major landmarks and the urban furniture reiterate the singular nature of Thames Town. At the same time, the skyscrapers of Songjiang New Town remain visible from various angles, interrupting the totalizing British ambience (Figure 31).

This striking contrast fascinates those who own homes in Thames Town, for whom entering the village generates particular enthusiasm. "When I enter Thames Town I always feel a little excited. I know I am home, and I remember that we live in England every day," says Deshi, the fifty-eight-year-old owner of a 480 m² villa in Hampton Garden who moved there from Sydney, Australia, in 2007. Qiao, a sixty-one-year-old resident of Rowland Heights, remembers the first time he and his wife, Hui, toured the village. "We had visited other villa compounds. But this is better because the whole community is different . . . when you come from outside you know you are here," he told me once while crossing the "Thames River." "Can you see those?" he asked, pointing at the distant skyscrapers of Songjiang. "Those buildings all look the same . . . when I see them I remember how special we are . . . people who live there see us and think we are different. Then they come to see us."

Figure 31. The residential towers of Songjiang New Town visible from Thames Town.

And visitors do indeed come. Huilang, a thirty-one-year-old resident of Songjiang, drives to Thames Town twice a year with her boyfriend, Yang, a forty-five-year-old real estate executive, along with his sixteen-year-old daughter from a previous marriage. The three spend time in the downtown area before picnicking on the grass of the islands. The contrast between Thames Town and Songjiang is striking to them: "Everything is different here. For a few hours, I feel like we are away from home . . . when you walk around you get to visit England, for free." Huilang likes to prepare an "English meal" for this special occasion because she believes that complementing the ambience with food makes the day even better. Watching videos online, she learned to bake delicious chicken and vegetable pies with the electric oven that Yang bought for her as a present. (Baking is not part of Chinese traditional cuisine. For this reason, kitchens are not usually equipped with an oven, which is considered an exotic appliance.) After eating the pies, the family usually visits one of the local cafés to buy dessert. The whole experience is special for Huilang. "Sometimes you see the city far away, but that's ok. It makes you feel even better because it reminds you that you are in a special place."

The seemingly natural—but actually manmade—beauty of Thames Town also attracts many visitors. Especially during the weekend, anglers crowd the banks of the canals to pass a few peaceful hours. Some fishermen extend their visits to downtown Thames Town. Guangli, the forty-one-year-old owner of a photocopy shop in Songjiang, visits Thames Town every Saturday, for example. Fishing had been his favorite activity as a child, but it had been years since he had done it. When the British town was completed, Guangli could resume his hobby. Instead of parking close to the canal, he leaves his car downtown and walks through the village to reach his fishing spot. When asked why he did not park closer to the canal, he answered that traversing the town made the whole experience even more pleasant, making him feel not only like a Chinese fisherman but also like a tourist in a foreign country.

All users are aware that the Britishness of Thames Town was synthetically produced a few years ago, but it is precisely this awareness that enhances the excitement. "I feel like a princess. Even better than a Disney one. Here things are real because this village is real!" said Zhen, a twenty-three-year-old bride-to-be, whom I met with her partner, Xueqin, twenty-five, and their two-year-old boy. Both Zhen and Xueqin were born in Shanghai but had lived in Songjiang New Town for six years when I met them. "I came here with my friends to look at this place when they built it . . . I had never seen something like this before," Xueqin told me. When I asked how he felt about the fact that the "historic" environment was in fact brand new, Xueqin suggested that my question was pointless given that all cities had been built at some point and that "people visit them because they like them, not because they are old." "When people look at our pictures they won't be able to say whether or not we are in England for real. But I know I am in Shanghai. This makes things even funnier!" said

Lili, a twenty-two-year-old bride, holding hands with her fiancé, Guotin, who is twenty-four. The future bride and groom were both from Henan province, but they met in Shanghai, where they each had moved in search of jobs after finishing high school. When Guotin proposed after eleven months, Lili knew what she wanted: an English wedding like she had seen in the movies. "Today we are VIPs! England is the perfect place to get a fairy tale marriage . . . I feel like William and Kate."

Since they could only afford a mid-tier photo shoot, Lili and Guotin purchased a "four dresses package" from the Lili Salon, a little one-room business owned by a local lady and located at the core of Thames Town. Three out of four styles reflected Lili's passion for England: "Romantic modern," "Classic English," and "Classic European"; Lili also picked "Traditional Chinese" because her grandmother back home insisted on having a traditional picture of the bride and groom. "But I am here because of the church and the buildings," Lili specified. "If I wanted a Chinese wedding, I would do that home" (Figures 32 and 33).

Figure 32. Engaged couples with matching outfits: "Western Romantic," "Western Classic," and "Traditional Chinese."

Figure 33. An engaged couple inside the Milan salon, downtown.

Commercial activities in Thames Town simultaneously exploit and enhance the British atmosphere. Mrs. Li, the owner of the Lili Salon, opened her business in 2009. She entered the wedding industry after finding out that her friend who owned a salon in Songjiang had quadrupled her profits since Thames Town was completed.[2] The Lili Salon can serve up to fifteen couples a day—while the prestigious Milan Salon down the street can handle up to ninety. Mrs. Li, who used to have a clothing shop before opening Lili, watched a number of British and American movies before deciding what dresses and accessories to stock (Figure 34). "We need to be careful with what we give them [the clients] because they come prepared . . . they know what is English and want it that way." In 2011, she joined a group of colleagues for a trip to England. A local company had organized a tour of the most famous UK wedding destinations, concluding with a wedding fair in Manchester. Mrs. Li was deeply disappointed by the real England. Above all, she disliked that the historic cities used for the photo shoots were inhabited urban centers. This, Mrs. Li noticed, reduced the efficiency of the photography business because the photographers could not easily catch the right backdrop and ensure the absence of passersby in the frame. Mrs. Li was also dissatisfied by real England because she expected to see many more bride-and-groom couples in the British centers. Ultimately, to Mrs. Li Thames Town is as beautiful as—and more efficient than—its English counterparts.

Figure 34. Costumes hanging in the Lili wedding salon, downtown.

The presence of brides and grooms considerably influences the atmosphere of Thames Town. The tourists like to watch the engaged couples because they emphasize the exoticness of Thames Town. "They change their outfits and pose with the photographers . . . it feels like Hollywood," said the tourist Huilang, who has never traveled outside of China. "Being among them makes me wish I was a princess. I dream of my own wedding. . . . Maybe I will go to England by then," said Xiaoli, Huilang's stepdaughter. The business owners also welcome the couples' presence regardless of whether their businesses are related to the wedding industry. Jie, the owner of a downtown café popular for British-themed events, such as its Sunday brunch (Figure 35), believed that the presence of the couples boosted her profits. Without the wedding industry, she told us, Thames Town would sit empty: The Englishness of the place on its own was not enough to attract visitors. The spectacle of the couples provided a reason to visit and spend time (and money) in the village. "Maybe it's not really an English thing, but all these couples are funny to watch," Jie told me.

Figure 35. Jie's café, downtown.

If tourists and shop owners seem unanimously to appreciate the presence of the engaged couples, residents expressed conflicting feelings about them. Most interviewees were happy that the photography business had made Thames Town famous. But they also dislike the noise and dirt they believe the couples and their entourages produce. In the view of Meili, a fifty-six-year-old villa owner, the couples compromised the Britishness of Thames Town. In 2007, Meili and her husband, Deshi, moved back to China after spending fourteen years in Australia, where they owned a retail import-export company. By buying a villa in Thames Town, Meili and Deshi hoped to remain connected to the Western lifestyle they experienced in Sydney's suburbs. "When we bought this house they [real estate agents] promised us the same life we had in Australia. This [Thames Town] is beautiful and looks like England, but it's not."

At the top of Meili's list of disappointments were the fitness center's inadequate machinery and limited opening hours—their local gym in Australia operated 24/7, but the one in Thames Town is only open between 10 am and 6 pm. Meili's second greatest disappointment in Thames Town was that downtown did not function as an English village. Meili had never traveled to the United Kingdom. But having lived in Australia, she felt she knew what it was like. "There are no good restaurants here, it's boring, everything closes too early . . . this is not like England, I know that." In Meili's view, the couples were the ultimate proof that Thames Town was anything but British: "They change clothes too often and some of their outfits are not suited to a wedding . . . this does not happen in England."

This awareness that Thames Town was not accurately or ideally providing a "Western" environment did not prevent Meili and Deshi from furnishing their home in a "British" fashion, like most residents of Thames Town. When Qiao and Hui bought their Rowland Heights villa, they were eager to experience England to its fullest extent. "We asked the design firm for the classic Western style because it's the most suitable for this village," said Hui, who spent eight months picking her English furniture (Figure 36). Qiao and Hui are especially proud of their basement living room, for which they commissioned a wooden bar counter from the Shanghai branch of a European design firm. Full of expensive Western liqueurs that Quaio and Hui do not drink, the counter stands beside an unused billiard table: "I ordered this from a European factory because I wanted a real one," Qiao told me. "I know it was probably made in China!" Next door, the ping-pong room is the only space in the basement that Qiao and Hui actually use on a daily basis (Figure 37). Other residents also commonly fill their homes with objects they believe to be English. "Thames Town is the closest thing to England we can afford," said Chuhao, forty-five, the owner of a 90 m² apartment in Kensington Garden that he and his wife themed like a boat, complete with a white-and-red life preserver hanging on the wall.

Figure 36. Qiao and Hui sitting in their living room.

Figure 37. Qiao and Hui's basement, with a billiard table. In a separate room is a ping-pong table.

Residents appropriate and resignify Western symbols in inventive ways. A number of villa owners, for example, mounted Christian crosses on the facades of their homes. When asked why, these residents said that the crucifix was a Western adornment that matched the Gothic church downtown but that it had no religious implications for them. This was not surprising, considering that the shop in front of the church downtown sold Catholic items as part of its evocation of a British atmosphere, even though Britain is an overwhelmingly Protestant country. Hanghui and Jia, a retired couple who own a villa on Windsor Island, chose to decorate their home in the style of the American architect Frank Lloyd Wright, an option that their interior design firm had offered along with "Tudor," "Victorian," and "Mies Van Der Rohe." The brick fireplace,

Figure 38. Hanghui and Jia's living room, designed in the "Frank Lloyd Wright Style."

Figure 39. A 1930s-like lamp and a reproduction of Gustav Klimt's The Kiss complete the "Frank Lloyd Wright Style."

the chandeliers and lamps of dark metal and glass, and the dark wood balustrade effectively recalled a modern American living room (Figures 38 and 39). A few feet away, a decorative plate mounted on the kitchen wall prescribed the recipe for a "Happy Home." Stickers of the Teletubbies and Santa Claus adorned the plaque, which the owners were unable to read. Although Hanghui and Jia do not speak English, they bought the plate in a local shop because "it was English." Their grandchildren later added the stickers for the same reason (Figure 40).

All residents kept a British theme in mind when decorating their homes. Not everyone, however, picked a décor in harmony with the theme: Some residents wanted their Chinese interiors to contrast with their exterior façades. "I think it is funny that you expect to find something English, and you enter here instead," remarked Hualing, the forty-seven-year-old owner of a 480 m² villa in Hampton Garden. She and her husband live separately but own three other units together in the Shanghai metropolitan area.

Figure 40. A Teletubbies decorative plaque hanging in Hanghui and Jia's kitchen.

Hualing lives in Thames Town along with their fifteen-year-old son, who attends the local international school. Her husband, a high-ranking executive in a German corporation, stays in their apartment in the Hongqiao district.

Hualing liked Thames Town especially for its English appearance, greenery, international school, and community of residents. The interiors of Hualing's house contrasted sharply with its Western-style exteriors. The layout, furniture pieces, and hanging paintings were exquisitely Chinese (Figures 12 and 41). Sitting on a hanmdmade chair in her tearoom, Hualing told us that she wouldn't have felt at ease living in a Western-style home. After all, this was the kind of house she had dreamed of as a child. But Hualing's preference for Chinese interiors also reflected a preoccupation with patriotism. Although China's recent marketizing turn had greatly benefited Hualing's family, she was concerned that an excessive glorification of the West—particularly America—

Figure 41. The Chinese interiors of Hualing's villa.

would make people forget indigenous culture: "Chinese traditions must not be forgotten . . . all of my other houses in Shanghai look Chinese like this one."

Daiyu and her husband, Tengfei, also chose to style their house in a Chinese fashion. Both in their sixties, husband and wife were among the first to move into Rowland Heights. Although Daiyu and Tengfei were glad that the British atmosphere had made their town unique and famous, they did not feel like changing the ways they lived indoors. They filled their home with Chinese furniture pieces and adjusted its layout according to the principles of fengshui (Figure 42). Daiyu was very proud of the contrast between the outdoors and indoors of their home. In her view, this contrast symbolized the power to choose, a right for which she and her husband had worked hard as employees of the City of Shanghai before retiring to Thames Town. Daiyu and Tengfei were

Figure 42. The Chinese interiors of Daiyu and Tengfei's villa.

able to purchase their villa by combining their life savings with a mortgage. Their son Sying, a thirty-four-year-old executive in a Chinese banking group, lived in Shanghai and visited on weekends. Sying told me that he saw his father cry for the first time when his parents moved into their villa. "This was unimaginable when I was a child," said Sying. And since the unimaginable had occurred, Daiyu and Tengfei were determined to make it work. Daiyu was a leading member of her residential community. Every day, she took walks through the gated area, making sure that Rowland Heights was maintaining its aesthetic and orderly standards. When I asked why she did not do the same in the downtown area, she told me that she did not like to mix with the people who were there. She and her husband had moved to Thames Town to be able finally to live quietly. To Daiyu, confining herself to the gated areas was the greatest form of freedom.

The visitors, engaged couples, and residents of Thames Town simultaneously consume and construct the British atmosphere. The singular nature of Thames Town generates enthusiasm among these groups. The residents are proud of the exclusive community they inhabit, and they consciously play with its theme when furnishing their homes. The atmosphere of the village triggers the enchantment of the engaged couples, who comfortably switch outfits from Western to Chinese. The tourists appreciate Thames Town's mix of "natural" and built beauty, taking it in while enjoying European-like food and goods. The individuals of each group enhance one another's appreciation for Thames Town: The engaged couples attract the visitors, who in turn please the residents because they demonstrate the town's popularity. The presence of the theme thus triggers the enthusiasm of the town's users, who simultaneously consume and produce its unique atmosphere. This atmosphere, however, also affects the way people behave and ultimately excludes those who do not look or act in ways that fit with the theme.

THE CONTROLLING ASPECTS OF THE THEME

There is no hanging laundry to be seen in Thames Town. Nearly all townspeople avoid using outdoor clotheslines out of a sense of responsibility for the town's appearance. This attitude stands in sharp contrast with what one commonly sees in China, where clotheslines full of drying laundry are an omnipresent feature of most urban landscapes. Many residents of the terrace houses solved the clothesline "problem" by building glass walls around their balconies (Figure 43). Some villa owners found ways to dry clothes without compromising the facades of their houses. Daiyu, for example, the owner of the Chinese-furnished villa in Rowland Heights, dries her clothing in the garage. She used to hang washing out of the window in her old Shanghai apartment, but she stopped when she and Tengfei moved. Daiyu's choice was primarily motivated by the desire to keep the villa and its surroundings pristine. She was very proud of her influence on her neighbors, who followed her example. Indeed, residents often change their behaviors to imitate their neighbors. For instance, Jia, who did let her clothes dry outside when she moved into her Frank Lloyd Wright–style villa, changed her habits when her husband pointed out that no one else in Windsor Island was hanging laundry. Wife and husband went to a shop in the Hongqiao expats' district and bought a dryer. Jia did not like using the appliance, which in her view makes clothes crumpled and smelly. Still, she thought the dryer was worth using because at least she was no longer the only resident who did not know "the right way."

Figure 43. The terrace houses of Kensington Garden, with the glass walls on the balconies that hide laundry hanging to dry.

The residents also adjusted their indoor habits to preserve the appearance of their homes. The English layout and furniture did not always fit their needs, but they often confined themselves to areas of the house in which they felt comfortable, leaving the other, more "English" spaces empty. Various villa residents, for example, kept the open, Western-like kitchen only for appearances' sake and cooked their meals in another room. In Jia and Hanghui's villa, the first kitchen—with its British furniture and Teletubbies stickers—was immaculate. The oven—as mentioned, a rarity in Chinese houses, where cooking is normally done by steaming or frying—was used for storage. Jia felt more comfortable in the second kitchen, in the rear of the first floor, where she could cook without making the whole house smell like food.

The kitchens are not the only English rooms that stand empty in Thames Town. Before letting me photograph their beautiful basement, Qiao and Hui made sure to remove the plastic covers protecting their billiard table and bar. Although—or maybe because—they were so proud of that room, they barely used it. They told me that they did not really need the space, which was there solely to "make them happy." All the rooms on the third floor of Qiao and Hui's villa were furnished in a British style. Neither husband nor wife had ever slept in them, and they had not set foot in the rooms in months when they gave me a tour of their villa. Qiao and Hui spent most of their free time in a small living room furnished with cots, a table, chairs, and a TV stand. When I asked, Qiao would not allow me to take a picture of that room; it was not, he said, representative of life in Thames Town.

Most tourists share with the residents the desire to experience and preserve the themed atmosphere. As mentioned previously, some visitors prepared and consumed English-like food that they thought matched the ambience of Thames Town. They also engaged in other activities that seemed "Western" to them. The LEGO Educational Center downtown offered classes in English for children. Most of the parents that I met at the school came from Songjiang New Town and traveled weekly (about an hour) to take their children to Thames Town. Bohai, a thirty-six-year-old father, told me that he did not come to Thames Town because of the English classes—he could find plenty in his Songjiang neighborhood. Nor was Bohai particularly passionate about the famous Danish bricks. Rather, Bohai traveled an hour to take his son to the LEGO Educational Center because of its special location. He believed that the overall atmosphere of Thames Town made his son's learning experience more effective and complete.

The visitors actively avoid spoiling the ambience or behaving in ways that would not fit the Britishness of Thames Town. Most tourists with whom my assistant and I talked consciously chose not to sit, eat, or litter unless they found dedicated spaces for those activities. Plenty of visitors sat on the grassy areas of the islands, but they refrained from doing so on the green spaces downtown. Jiaying, a twenty-seven-year-old visitor to Thames Town, told us that she felt very comfortable on the grass of the island, where she was sunbathing when we approached her. In contrast, Jiaying thought that the grass in front of the church was not for sitting; it was there "to be looked at." When asked why she thought so, she said that the downtown's British-themed appearance required that people using the spaces be careful not to ruin it. Similarly, a tourist named Yang told us that he did not litter in the public spaces of downtown Thames Town, though he was accustomed to doing that in his own neighborhood. "If everybody used this place as they'd like, it wouldn't be the same," he said. Thus far, I have given examples of users who consciously change their behavior to conform to and preserve the British atmosphere as they imagine it. But the behavior of people in Thames Town is also subject to the control and repression of community managers and guards. The Residents' Committee Center, located behind the Municipal Square, is in charge of the town's rules, issuing and enforcing common requirements for keeping Thames Town safe, clean, and British. In reality, however, it was usually the residents with the most money and prestige who decided what rules should be established and enforced within their community.

The rules within the gated areas shifted at the discretion of the residents. The case of dog ownership in Leeds Garden is a good example. Although no written rule prohibited pets when I first visited Thames Town, the guards told me that residents had verbally agreed that no dogs were allowed in Leeds Garden. During my stay, however, this policy changed to the point that, by the end of my fieldwork, at least five villa owners had dogs. The view of the residents shifted, the guards explained to me, when a couple of particularly affluent retirees moved to the Leeds Garden community, bringing along two dogs. The arrival of the two dogs upset most residents, so the couple sought to soften the reaction by organizing a party, to which they invited their fellow residents, along with the couple's friends—who included some influential politicians from Shanghai. The new residents' display of affluence and power sufficed to prompt the community to change the rules on pet ownership overnight. The day after the party, the guards told us, three residents had gone to the porters' lodge, at different times, to let the guards know that from then on dogs were permitted in Leeds Garden.

COPING WITH THE THEME: EVERYDAY ADJUSTMENTS AND SPONTANEOUS APPROPRIATIONS

The rules established by the residents have produced a de facto segregation of the floating population of migrants who pass through Thames Town. As mentioned, the laborers employed in the construction business live in the village for about a year, customarily sleeping in the spaces they are renovating or squatting in nearby vacant units. The migrant workers often use outdoor spaces to cook or simply to rest after work, since the units they inhabit often lack running water or electricity. The residents of the gated clusters do not tolerate these behaviors because they do not want the workers—who usually come from rural areas—to be visible in their neighborhoods.

Most inhabitants thought that street vending, hanging laundry in public, or eating on the streets spoiled the Thames Town atmosphere. They thus ask the guards to reprimand anyone involved in these activities and eventually to expel those who persist. These measures segregate the migrant workers. The presence of the floating workers is tolerated differently by the various gated compounds. The residents of Windsor Island, for example, were particularly bothered by the workers' presence and asked the guards to walk through the compound and command the migrants to remain indoors. Xiaosi, a forty-seven-year-old guard on Windsor Island, told us that he enforced these rules only reluctantly. He felt particularly uneasy telling workers with children to keep their kids inside.

Life in Kensington Garden was relatively easier for the migrant workers because the residents allowed them to be visible in public (Figure 44). My assistant and I first met Huojin and Zihao in front of the terrace house they were renovating. Both were in their mid-fifties. They had left their rural village in Jiangsu province about ten years earlier and arrived in Shanghai in search of opportunities. When we met them, they had been living in Thames Town for about a year.

Figure 44. Hanging laundry and a bowl of vegetables left out by migrant workers squatting in Kensington Garden.

Although well integrated into the town's community of about two hundred migrant laborers, neither man had enjoyed living in Thames Town. In Kensington Garden, the two workers slept inside the construction site but spent most of their free time in front of the house (Figure 45). Huojin and Zihao explained to us that the possibility of spending leisure time within the gated areas was a privilege for them, since guards in other compounds would not allow that. This was the case in Hampton Garden, where the two had stayed before moving to Kensington. In Hampton Garden, villa residents and guards all reprimanded workers for smoking or hanging their laundry outside. Back then, the only place for Huojin and Zihao to relax was outside the gates of Hampton Garden or in the downtown residential areas. The situation was better in Kensington Garden, Huojin told us, because at least there nobody would tell them to remain inside.

Not surprisingly, neither Huojin nor Zihao liked Thames Town. In their view, the village was uncomfortable and too expensive.

Everything was too far away: There were no shops to buy food or conveniently located restaurants. Neither Huojin nor Zihao possessed any means of transportation and relied on their friends' scooter to go to Songjiang from time to time. They usually bought their food downtown, where other migrant workers cooked and sold meals for their peers.

Figure 45. The migrant workers Huojin and Zihao in a Kensington Garden unit.

The residential areas in Thames Town's downtown—where the occupancy rate was much lower than in the gated communities—were the only places where migrant workers can gather without being asked to leave. For this reason, some workers choose to occupy vacant units downtown on a permanent basis rather than move each time they finished renovating a unit. These workers walked to their worksites every morning and then returned downtown in the evening to sleep. Such squatting was risky, however.

Huojin and Zihao introduced me to a forty-nine-year-old migrant woman who resided downtown (Figure 13). She told me that a few months earlier, a group of owners had complained about the workers' presence in the Robin Apartments area. Guards subsequently entered three occupied apartments and threw away all of the migrants' appliances and furniture. Despite the constant risk of displacement, the migrant woman still thought it was worth occupying the downtown units. There, at least most of the time, she could cook, hang her laundry, and spend time outside without being constantly monitored. The woman lived in the Chelsea Garden area with her husband, daughter, son-in-law, and two-year-old grandchild. While the rest of the group worked in the construction business, she spent her time taking care of her daughter's child and three other migrants' small children. It remains unclear to me what form of compensation the woman received; although she did not want to tell us whether the other migrants paid her to take care of their children, she mentioned that her baby-sitting activity contributed to the well-being of the other members of the family.

For the migrant workers, the Western look of Thames Town was more of an added annoyance than a pleasant feature. The employment conditions in the British village were similar to those other workers received, in terms of payment and schedule. But there were also rules particular to Thames Town that the construction workers had to respect in order to remain employed. Before working in that village, the migrants had never been asked to avoid hanging their laundry, cooking, or being visible in public. These restrictions, they agreed, were the result of the town's exclusivity, which was inseparable from its particular appearance. Huojin and Zihao liked the shape of the buildings, the quietness, and greenery of the village. They were also amused by the spectacle of the wedding couples. Those pleasant features, however, were not appealing enough to make Huojin and Zihao want to live there.

Overall, the two workers felt uncomfortable in the British village. The residents of gated communities outside Thames Town had never been particularly hospitable toward the migrants, either. Yet Huojin and Zihao found the attitude of the Thames Town residents to be particularly hostile. The two workers explicitly associated the residents' sentiments toward the migrants with the British atmosphere of the town. They repeated multiple times that the affluent residents did not want the workers around because they thought that they spoiled the English atmosphere. In the view of the migrant workers, the Western character of Thames Town symbolized above all the constricting rules they were forced to follow.

Not all the people who were in Thames Town behaved according to the rules established by the residents. Some users challenged the regulations by using the spaces as they saw fit, even if their activities interfered with the crafted atmosphere. Engaged couples who could not afford a wedding salon, for example, would hire a photographer and a makeup artist and use the sidewalks as their dressing room. The presence of these "do-it-yourself" couples annoyed the managers of the wedding salons, who asked the guards to expel them from the streets. In most cases, such couples ignored the guards (Figures 45 and 46).

I once saw a bride who, getting dressed on the street, refused to move when a guard asked her to. The bride said that she was as entitled to be there as anyone else in the town. As she saw it, there was no difference between posing, getting dressed, or eating on the street. After all, she said, Thames Town existed to be visited, and visitors could do what they wanted. The brides who were using a local salon were also supporting the presence of the do-it-yourself couples for different reasons. Lili, the twenty-two-year-old bride who wore a Chinese dress only to please her grandmother, told me that the presence of less affluent brides signaled her privileged and more affluent status. "They [the do-it-yourself couples] remind me of how much we have worked to be here today," she said. But other couples also encourage the presence of brides and grooms in the streets because they believe it is "fair." For example, Zhen, the twenty-three-year-old bride who praised Thames Town for its "realness," told us that the English village should be accessible to all, as other cities are. Just because Thames Town was "special," she thought, should not mean that people must have money to use it.

For their part, the guards maintained an ambiguous and ambivalent attitude toward enforcing the rules. On the one hand, they obeyed the orders of the residents and business owners, who in turn gave the guards tips. At the same time, some guards also

Figure 46. "Do-it-yourself" couples getting ready for their photo shoots on the sidewalks of downtown Thames Town.

Figure 47. "Do-it-yourself" couples getting ready for their photo shoots on the sidewalks of downtown Thames Town.

transgressed the very rules they were supposed to enforce. A few, for example, slept in the porters' lodges or squatted in vacant units downtown. Some also participated in the informal vending trade, selling products to the migrant workers.

As mentioned earlier, the migrant workers cannot easily commute from Songjiang. To buy food and other necessities, they rely on street vendors who come to town in the evening. The residents believe that street commerce compromises the atmosphere of the village and ask the guards to drive the vendors out. This did not stop the informal commerce, however, which continued out of the residents' sight. The guards not only failed to expel the vendors; some even became directly involved in the vending business. Weimin, a forty-nine-year-old guard, traded food out of the Kensington Garden porter's lodge. He had started the practice a year earlier in another gated area, but he shut down and moved the business after the residents of that compound complained. Two nights a week, Weimin stocked the lodge with fruits and vegetables and waited for workers from nearby units. Other vendors also gathered in front of those gates, transforming the space into a small informal night market.

The gates and porters' lodges that were meant for surveillance thus ironically became spaces where migrants and guards together spent time breaking the rules. Although the guards believed they occupied a higher rung on the social ladder than the migrants, they persistently demonstrated sympathy toward the workers. Chung, a fifty-two-year-old colleague of Weimin, told us that he considered the guards a group in between the wealthy residents and the migrant workers. For this reason, Chung thought that the guards of Thames Town were caught in a tension. On the one hand, they aspired to one day be like the villa owners they worked for, while on the other hand the guards equally understood the needs of the workers. Weimin told us that, beyond obvious reasons of profit, he maintained his informal business because his trade made life easier for the migrants. "We [guards] understand how they [migrant workers] feel. I was a migrant myself," Weimin told us, referring to when ten years ago he lived in the center of Shanghai, working at a friend's shop.

In a logic of "us" and "them," the guards selectively elect to include or exclude the workers from their own group. In some instances, the guards refer to the migrants as fellow workers who, just like the wardens, live separately from and must cope with "them": the rich residents. The guards often mentioned the lack of affordable services and housing as problems that they shared with the migrants and something that created solidarity among the two groups. At the same time, however, the migrants represent an annoyance for the guards. The wardens are in part upset because their employers complain about the migrants' visibility and that the guards do not always manage to enforce the rules. But the migrants' presence also bothers the guards because they see the construction workers as rustic peasants that spoil the atmosphere. Expressing this feeling, the guards referred to themselves as urban dwellers who, just like the wealthy residents, had to cope with "them": the dirty workers. Chung, for example, showed mixed feelings of respect, envy, and—at times—anger toward the residents and told us that the migrants could understand his sentiments. At the same time, however, Chung supported the residents' disapproval of the migrants, who in his view did give a bad look to Thames Town. Chung had not always thought this way. When he started working in the village, Chung did not care about its "Britishness." With time, however, he began to appreciate the unique atmosphere, and he did not want it spoiled.

In these ways, the ordinary activities taking place in Thames Town simultaneously reiterate and contest the controlling aspects of the themed environment. My observations, questionnaires, and interviews revealed that the presence of the theme affected the ways people behaved in the space. The British motif functioned as a cohesive device because it prompted residents and visitors to modify their behavior willingly in order to construct and preserve the themed atmosphere. Contextually, the theme also led to the segregation of the migrant workers who did not conform to the town's aesthetic and behavioral codes.

These circumstances demonstrate that the symbolism of the British theme enabled and sustained explicit and implicit mechanisms of control. However, ordinary behaviors also complicated the single dominant image of Thames Town because individuals interpreted and used the Britishness of the village in different ways. Indeed, some users violated the rules established by the residents and engaged with the spaces according to their own needs and desires, using Thames Town as a stage for their own spontaneous and provisional appropriations.

ENDNOTES

1.   During my fieldwork, I found that less than a third of the units in downtown Thames Town and about half of the units in the gated areas were occupied. In February 2013, the office manager at the Thames Town Community Center told me that the village housed two thousand residents by then. Henriot and Minost (2017) report that there were 2,300 residents in 2014. Given that the community was designed to house ten thousand residents, this means that Thames Town is occupied at less than one-fourth of its capacity.

2.   Wedding salons located in Songjiang New Town organize minivan trips to Thames Town. Future brides and grooms get ready in Songjiang and then travel to Thames Town with the photographers and hairstylists. Later in the day, the minivan functions as a rehearsal space where the couples change dresses and styles. Songjiang wedding salons usually offer services for two-thirds the price of a Thames Town business.

CHAPTER 4

The Spaces Authenticity Makes

AUTHENTICITY AS A DYNAMIC RELATIONSHIP

The crowded themed core, exclusive gated communities, vacant units, and occasional night markets of Thames Town all seem to differ greatly from one another. Yet, I argue, the spaces of Thames Town are similar because these are the spaces that authenticity makes. Notions of authenticity govern the creation, consumption, and contestation of all of Thames Town's places, no matter how their uses and users diverge. Scholars of tourism and heritage insist that authenticity is not a finite quality but rather a relational condition. People establish this condition within themselves and with their surroundings by living, sensing, and at times contesting space. These dynamics are apparent in Thames Town, which at once produces and is produced by its users' ideas of "the authentic."

The notion of authenticity inherently contains ambiguity. The word "authentic" generally designates aspirations of true identity, genuineness, and originality. I believe that three typologies of authenticity are particularly relevant to the contemporary urban experience. Moral authenticity refers to the condition of being, and aspiring to be, true to oneself (Heidegger 1996 [1927]); material authenticity is the veracity of an artifact that is central to theories and practices of preservation (Jokilehto 1995); and symbolic authenticity is the sentiment that consumers seek through the experience of images and places (Knudsen and Waade, 2010). These three kinds of authenticity are all different, but they all involve a tension between continuity and change. We perceive this tension when the world we inhabit changes too rapidly. The more things around us are altered, the more we long for what is gone—and for what possibly never quite existed the way we remember it.

Indeed, concerns over "the authentic" emerged together with the socioeconomic transformations of modern Europe over the past several centuries. During that period, the copy acquired a negative connotation, and a need for sincerity undergirded the moral condemnation of fakery (Trilling 1972). As a reaction to the profound changes Western societies underwent during the industrial revolutions, the quest for authenticity arose as "one of the most politically explosive of modern impulses" (Berman 1970, xxvii). The desire for authenticity has gained even greater ascendancy since the 1970s, when the pursuit of "the authentic" became one of the driving forces behind the experience economy. Authenticity has then emerged, especially in the last three decades, as a potent branding tool that motivates consumers and favors the attraction of capital (Banet-Weiser 2012; Gilmore and Pine 2007).

Scholars of urban studies are increasingly aware that the consumer quest for authenticity affects how cities are produced and consumed around the world. One hears the word "authenticity" frequently in discussions of urban regeneration, diversity, and gentrification. Yet in most cases, scholars use the term elusively. At times, they refer to authenticity as an asset, as the quality of an "original" place or community that architects and planners need to protect. At other times, urbanists associate authenticity with the production of Disneyfied landscapes of consumption that control citizens and exclude vulnerable groups. Part of this ambiguity is justified by the fact that authenticity is indeed an equivocal concept entangled simultaneously with notions of authority and resistance. However, I am convinced that authenticity persists as an omnipresent yet vague notion in urban studies because we have not yet systematically analyzed *how authenticity actually functions* in the city.

The sociologist Sharon Zukin (2009) suggests that authenticity provides an analytical model for interpreting the production and transformation of the landscapes of power. She also calls attention to the ways in which authenticity involves both mechanisms of dominance and practices of resistance. On the one hand, authenticity is an elitist category of aesthetic judgment that affects consumer taste and reinforces dominant narratives of growth. Influential actors appeal to people's quests for the authentic in order to produce and profit from city making. Claims of authenticity, however, can also demand "a right to the city, a human right that is cultivated by long time residence, use, and habit" (Zukin 2010, 244). This occurs, for example, when ethnic minorities or "social preservationists" use the notion of authenticity to "preserve group solidarity, prevent displacement and ease inter-group tensions" (Zukin 2009, 545). Urbanists have studied how this ambivalence of authenticity manifests itself in the city. They have looked at how the pursuit of "the authentic" underlies phenomena such as gentrification (Brown-Saracino 2009; Zukin 2008), preservation and place making (Jive'n and Larkham 2003; Ouf 2001), the commodification of ethnic diversity (Rath 2007; Shaw et al. 2004), and the Disneyfication of touristic centers (Judd and Fainstein 1999).

From these studies, it has now become common to suggest that ideas of authenticity guide urban phenomena such as gentrification, preservation, and place. However, scholars have not yet systematically looked at the kinds of social and spatial relationships that emerge because of the ways in which people construct and negotiate values of authenticity. That is, we have given little attention, if any, to how authenticity actually works as a process of urban change that determines the physical and social production of space.

Scholars of heritage and tourism have discussed more analytically the role that authenticity plays in our everyday experiences. Beginning in the 1970s, academic conversations developed two opposing approaches: objectivism and constructivism. While the former holds that only the artifacts that are original in their physical substance are authentic, the latter interprets authenticity as a social construct that depends on the cultural lens of the observer. Those supporting the objectivist view conceptually rooted their arguments in the modern condemnation of copies and in a generalized skepticism toward the culture industry (Benjamin 2008 [1936]; Horkheimer and Adorno 2002 [1944]). Objectivists then argued that authenticity is an inherent, non-negotiable, and verifiable property. In tourism studies, Dean MacCannell (1973, 1976) laid the theoretical foundations of objectivism, coining the term staged authenticity. Using Erving Goffman's analysis of social life, MacCannell interpreted contemporary mass tourism as being articulated between "front" and "back" regions and argued that tourists are alienated modern subjects who seek their true self through the experience of "an Other" culture. Searching "the authentic," tourists try to visit both the front and the back regions of places to have a real encounter with native people and cultures. But no matter how hard they try, MacCannel argues, modern tourists cannot escape being deceived because the destinations they visit are inevitably packaged with both front and back stages, and this conveys a false sense of authenticity.

The objectivist argument that the authenticity of an artifact cannot be faked informed the Eurocentric approaches to heritage preservation that most practitioners continue to follow around the world. The Venice Charter of the International Council of Monuments and Sites (ICOMOS 1964) established the "common responsibility" of governments to safeguard "ancient monuments" and hand them on to future generations "in the full richness of their authenticity" (art. 1). Authenticity in this context was strictly dependent on the material originality of an artifact. The chart stipulated that no intervention could be done unless it remained reversible and visible. Reconstructions and integrations should be distinguishable from the authentic and original parts of the monument in order to respect the artifact's historical and artistic authenticity (Brandi 2005). By the late 1970s, cultural properties could be listed in the World Heritage List only if they met the "Test of Authenticity." Still today, this test decides whether artifacts are genuine in terms of location, design, materials, use and function, traditions and techniques, and spirit and feeling (Stovel 1995).

In contrast to the objectivists, constructivists argued that people make their own interpretations of the authentic without necessarily being deceived by the culture industry. Constructed authenticity then is not exclusive to originals, but rather it transcends the materiality of artifacts. According to the constructivist view, users gradually construct and negotiate values of authenticity depending on their beliefs and expectations. It is the very experience of tourism, constructivists tell us, that allows people to develop sentiments of authenticity regardless of the material originality of the toured object. In the constructivist view, even reproductions can "become" authentic through the visitors' physical and emotional involvement (Bruner 2001; Cohen 1988; Pearce and Moscardo 1986; Redfoot 1984).

The constructivist idea that authenticity transcends material originality has also found support in preservation discourses. Both the ICOMOS Nara Document (1994) and the UNESCO Convention for the Safeguarding of the Intangible Cultural Heritage (2003) institutionalized the constructivist shift in heritage preservation. While the former acknowledges that judgments of authenticity rely on diverse cultural parameters, the latter holds that patterns of creativity, expertise, and knowledge must guide the recognition of authenticity as much as—and in some cultural contexts even more than—the material substance of an artifact (Kirshenblatt-Gimblett 2004; Kuutma 2015; Larsen 1995; Munjeri 2004). The Nara Document and the Convention on Intangible Heritage signaled a shift from a European-centered approach. This shift acknowledged that the traditional ways in which people maintain the authenticity of artifacts in Asian contexts diverge from what the UNESCO guidelines suggested. In most East Asian regions, it is the visual integrity and not the physical substance that makes artifacts "authentic." This fact explains, for example, why preservation coincides with complete reconstruction in Japan (Ito 1995) and why a copy can be as valuable as the "original" in the Chinese context (Weiler 2016; Zhu 2016).

The dichotomy between constructivism and objectivism has progressively thawed since the 2000s. Critics have agreed that both approaches offer only a partial interpretation of authenticity. The Objectivist positions give too much importance to the artifacts' materiality and underestimate the cultural components that inform users' appreciation of authenticity. Likewise, constructivists undervalue the importance of physicality in tourist experiences when they argue that the value of authenticity is independent from the concrete experience of places and goods (Holtorf 2013; Jones 2010). Researchers have also acknowledged that an exclusive focus on the definition of authenticity distracts them from more fruitful explorations. Decades of debate on what should and should not be considered authentic has prevented scholars from analyzing the sociopolitical implications of authenticity (Vannini 2011).

We should then explore what authenticity *does* rather than endlessly speculate on what authenticity *is*. Coined by Ning Wang (1999), the concept of "existential authenticity" signals this awareness. Wang theorized authenticity as a "potential state of being" that people activate when they consciously experience the liminality of tourist experiences. Although perceptions of authenticity "often have nothing to do with the issue of whether toured objects are real" (359), they are nonetheless deeply ingrained in people's material experience of the world. Following Wang, researchers understand authenticity as a condition at once detached from the materiality of the toured object yet embedded in it. Britta Timm Knudsen and Anne Marit Waade (2010) propose the notion of "performative authenticity" to describe a relational quality that individuals attribute to their surroundings through corporeal and affective practices. Authenticity, they argue, is neither exclusively related to individuals nor to the objects they look at. Rather, performative authenticity "has to do with what happens in between these two instances" (13). Along these lines, researchers have closely examined how the experience of the world informs our understanding of authenticity. They have especially argued that we authenticate places and objects through performative practices and that individual agency is essential to feeling, thinking, and rethinking the values of authenticity (Rickly-Boyd 2013; Smith and Cambel 2015; Zhu 2012).

More than a finite attribute, authenticity is a relational, dynamic, practice-related condition that emerges when individuals engage with the world that surrounds them. The implications of authenticity remain confined neither to the level of the individual nor to tourism experiences. Our perceptions of the authentic inform our "everyday assessments of social worth" and determine changes at both the personal and collective levels (Pearce and Moscardo 1986, 122). The systems of values that people associate with the notion of authenticity influence how societies work. Indeed, as Regina Bendix (1997) suggests, the idea of cultural authenticity "has become such convenient fodder" that it drives "political debates on race, ethnicity, gender, and multiculturalism" (9). Authenticity then influences how people live and interact with one another.

We can thus interpret authenticity as a relationship that individuals establish with the city through spatial and emotional experiences. The values that people attribute to authenticity affect the production, consumption, and contestation of urban spaces. Within this system, powerful actors produce and control landscapes by capitalizing on the values entailed by the idea of authenticity. Yet at the same time, the quest for the authentic also encourages negotiations and spontaneous appropriations of space by the less powerful. All of these dynamics are especially evident in Thames Town.

AUTHENTICITY AND THE PRODUCTION OF SPACE

By interpreting authenticity as a dynamic relationship between people, places, and meanings that generates urban transformation, I suggest that authenticity underlies the production of space as theorized by Henri Lefebvre (1991 [1974]). The French philosopher taught us that space is at once socially constructed and constitutive of social relationships and that a city's users participate in the production of space through their everyday lives. As mentioned earlier, the production of space concerns not only the physical organization of environments but also the negotiation and possible subversion of social relationships. The production of space is, then, a process that connects three dimensions: conceived, perceived, and lived spaces. Conceived space is the dominant space that materializes the mental and creative constructs that architects, urbanists, and scientists represent through symbols and rules. Perceived space is the concrete environment we experience through daily spatial practices. Finally, lived space includes and expands the perceived and the conceived dimensions. It is the dominated space that we inhabit but that we also contest and transform in our everyday lives. The Lefebvrian trialectics of space, comprised by the perceived-conceived-lived dimensions, is not an abstract product but rather an oeuvre: a work that is constantly produced through bodily and emotionally contingent practices.

The social, political, and economic implications of authenticity affect, and are affected by, the trialectics of space. They become concrete in the city through both top-down and bottom-up dynamics. The top-down/conceived dimensions materialize when powerful actors use the aesthetics of authenticity to produce and control landscapes. Developers, architects, and planners fulfill consumers' expectations by emplacing a dominant conception of "the authentic." The individuals who do not look or act "properly" remain excluded from the landscapes of commodified authenticity. As discussed in Chapter 2, themed settings typify these exclusionary ramifications. But authenticity also underlies the production of space through bottom-up processes and thus produces perceived and lived spaces. This occurs, for example, when the landscapes of tourism create economic opportunities for the poor, who exploit the staged authenticity in order to make a living (Bromley 1998; Crossa 2009), or when disenfranchised groups fight displacement by leveraging their history in a place—they being the "authentic" residents who have a right to stay (Brown-Saracino 2009; Zukin 2009). More pertinently to this work, given that individuals' ideas of "the authentic" inform how they interpret and behave in space, everyday practices related to sentiments of authenticity complicate dominant landscapes and produce specific politics of belonging.

In Thames Town, the potency of authenticity materializes in its top-down and bottom-up qualities. The conceived/dominant connotation of authenticity is evident in the Chinese village when we consider that developers and designers constructed an identifiably "authentic" British atmosphere in order to attract consumers. But the notion of authenticity—the ways people cope with the Englishness, construct their own meanings, and bypass the rules induced by the theme—also determines the production of perceived and lived spaces. If the themed atmosphere normalizes aesthetic and moral criteria that influence how people behave, it also encourages the spontaneous appropriations that make Thames Town the unique place that it is.

I reached these conclusions by analyzing the daily habits and perceptions of four groups of Thames Town users: the residents, the tourists, the engaged couples who use the village as the backdrop for their wedding photos, and the employees—security guards as well as the construction workers who live in Thames Town while they renovate its buildings. Observation, survey questionnaires, and interviews allowed me to investigate how the presence of the theme affects users' behaviors in both the free-access mixed-use downtown and the six gated communities. I especially looked at how the users of Thames Town engaged with space and how their sentiments toward the theme affected these dynamics. My fieldwork revealed that while all users adapt the various spaces of Thames Town according to their needs and aspirations, the symbolism of the built environment influences the spatial habits of diverse groups in different ways.

Ideas of authenticity—the desire to enjoy and preserve the Englishness of Thames Town but also the need to not interfere with such Englishness in order to avoid punishment—prevent different groups from overlapping in spaces. While the public areas downtown are crowded with the tourists and the engaged couples who together consume and fabricate the British atmosphere, the same areas are generally avoided by the residents. Proud of their exclusive community, the residents confine themselves within the gated clusters so as not to mix with other groups. The affluent inhabitants also ask the guards to expel migrant workers who hang laundry in public, eat on the streets, or simply sit outside the units that they are renovating. Forbidden to make themselves visible inside the gated communities, the workers gather outside the fences or squat in the vacant units downtown. The guards also tend to avoid the most iconic spaces, where they feel "constrained," and only overlap with tourists and residents if required by their duties.

Authenticity unites people when the tourists, the residents, and the couples behave in order to preserve and construct the English atmosphere. The residents at once enjoy and enhance the Englishness when they furnish their homes consciously playing with the theme. Some dwellers decorate their interiors in an English style, appropriating Western symbols—Frank Lloyd Wright interiors, wooden European-like bar counters, Teletubbies plates. Other residents pick Chinese décor either because they want to express their patriotism or because they are proud to have the power and money to choose an indoor atmosphere antithetical to the outdoors one. The staged authenticity of the village also triggers the playfulness of the engaged couples, who pose in front of the professional photographers and change easily into different outfits, both Western and Chinese. Willing to live the Britishness at its best, tourists purchase or bring from home European food to make their experience more "real." The couples, visitors, and residents enhance one another's appreciation for Thames Town: The engaged couples attract the visitors, whose presence pleases the residents because it proves that the town is popular.

The moral and aesthetic values that people attribute to "the authentic" have repercussions on how people behave and, ultimately, exclude the powerless. Most residents and visitors abstain from acting in ways they consider inappropriate. This is evident, for example, when most residents avoid hanging their laundry outside or when the tourists only sit, eat, or dispose of trash if they find urban furniture designated for those activities. The constructed authenticity of Thames Town also enables the exclusion of those individuals who look "out of place." The migrant workers do who do not behave according to the residents' standards must find "residual" noniconic spaces to spend time. In the view of the migrants, the British theme is mainly an annoyance that restricts their freedom and deprives Thames Town of affordable services. The guards maintain a more ambiguous attitude toward the theme. Some show sentiments of solidarity with the workers, with whom they share a mix of respect, envy, and fear toward the residents. At the same time, the wardens, whose job is to discipline the town, are disciplined by the residents and end up appropriating the same rhetorics of authenticity as their employers. The guards who have been working in Thames Town since its opening are preoccupied with preserving its Englishness than their recently hired colleagues. When asked, these guards told me that while initially they did not care, with time they developed an appreciation for the British atmosphere, which they do not want to be spoiled by "improper" users.

But both the constructed authenticity of Thames Town and the rules imposed in order to maintain such authenticity also create the very conditions for appropriations that disrupt the staged atmosphere. These appropriations occur because of the theme, in that users act either to enjoy the Britishness or to not interfere with it. When the engaged couples use the streets as dressing rooms and refuse to move when asked by the guards, for example, they do so because they appreciate the Englishness of Thames Town. Through their appreciation, however, the "do-it-yourself" couples also disturb the crafted authenticity and complicate its landscapes. The migrant workers circumnavigate the rules imposed by residents in order to avoid punishment and use the spaces freely. As they cannot stay visible in the most iconic spaces, the only way for the migrants to spend time outside is to go to the edges of the gated communities or to squat in the residential areas downtown. The lack of tourists and residents in these areas allows the migrant workers to manifest their presence by hanging their laundry, eating outside, and engaging in informal commerce at night. Street vending takes place in front of the gated areas, where, unbeknownst to the residents, the guards sell migrants goods and vegetables. When the wardens and the migrants organize the markets on the streets, they pick locations where they know the residents will not bother them, because the market will not compromise the "authentic" British look. Thus, paradoxically, the gates and porters' lodges intended to be spaces of control are where control is loosest in town because the theme is absent.

Each space of Thames Town has different uses and users. The touristic downtown is crowded with engaged couples and visitors. The residential clusters are inhabited by the nouveaux riches. Migrant workers who also populate the temporary street markets occasionally occupy the spectral Potemkin downtown. Despite their differences, all these spaces exist and coexist because the notion of authenticity underlies their production. Authenticity simultaneously includes and excludes the users of Thames Town by creating a specific politics of belonging. The system of values that users associate with the "authentic Britishness" of the village influences how people behave and thus determines how they shape and reshape Thames Town.

Even if notions of "real" and "fake" are elusive, the moral and aesthetic judgments we associate with them have concrete repercussions. The search for "authentic" experiences influences how we travel, consume, and reside around the world. Our aspirations of authenticity affect the existence of many, including those individuals who cannot choose where and how to live and are left to bear the consequences of other people's preferences. Thames Town is but one example of how powerful actors exploit authenticity to create exclusionary spaces. By selling the authentic, urban managers promote renewals, historic preservations, and themed developments that dislocate and segregate vulnerable groups worldwide. Yet authenticity also enables a city's users to produce space because it creates specific politics of belonging. As a dynamic relationship that people establish with their surroundings, authenticity controls a city's users but also encourages spatial appropriations and meaning making. This ambivalence challenges speculative—and Western centric—assumptions of what is "real" and what is "fake." At once an instrument of dominance and a trigger to self-expression, authenticity enables people to appropriate and transform the real fakes of this world.

Acknowledgments

I started thinking about *The Real Fake* during my PhD in Architecture and Urbanism at IUAV University of Venice. I am deeply thankful to the faculty who advised me there, especially Maria Chiara Tosi, Margherita Turvani, and Enrico Fontanari. As a visiting researcher at the Tongji University of Shanghai, I met many scholars to whom I am grateful. Li Xiangning provided much needed support by sharing ideas and helping me to organize the fieldwork. Lan Wang was a great friend and source of guidance. Shao Yong and my colleagues at the Office of Preservation at the Tongji Urban Planning and Design Institute taught me a lot. Harry den Hartog was incredibly generous and provided me with precious materials. I also want to express my gratitude to Daniel Monti, who made *The Real Fake* possible.

At the University of Southern California, I have the privilege to be inspired by an incredibly vibrant, diverse, and stimulating community of faculty members. I am grateful to the faculty of the Price School of Public Policy—Annette Kim, Dowell Myers, Lisa Schweitzer, and David Sloane—who provided me with sophisticated, thoughtful, and challenging advice. Alison Dundes Renteln was always insightful and supportive. Vanessa Schwartz and the people of the Visual Studies Research Institute made my intellectual journey surprising and wonderful.

My colleagues are brilliant, and I feel very lucky to call them friends. Sharing our vulnerabilities makes us stronger every day. The "Gateway crew" is fantastic. My cohort mates Soyoon Choo, Julia Harten, and Madi Swayne are but a few of the terrific people who make my daily life better. Up on the hills, at UCLA, Aaron Cayer was a wonderful, always cheerful roommate and companion. Huê-Tâm Webb Jamme is a great friend with whom I share fears, hopes, and a lot (a lot!) of laughs.

Tridib Banerjee is the most generous, wise, and thoughtful advisor I could ask for. I already knew of his legendary wisdom when I arrived at USC, but I could not imagine the mythical patience he showed by dealing with my passionate self. I would not be here if it wasn't for Anastasia Loukaitou-Sideris. Her integrity and generosity inspire and guide me. I am grateful to Tridib and Anastasia in ways I cannot describe in words—and, as anyone knows, I am never at a loss for words.

The people I love across the world are my strength. My grandmother Lydia is an anti-fascist lawyer to whom I owe a lot. I am thankful to my parents and brothers who did all they could to let me be here. Back in the Lithuania days, Dalius Vrublauskas questioned my assumptions on authenticity along with other certitudes that I left behind. Carla Conti is a warm, wise presence. Elisa Maceratini is the strongest woman I know and she never stops impressing me. Giulia Barbarossa knows all my "trash" secrets, from Mamiani's courtyard to M's passion. Giorgia Castagnoli and I met in Paris only to find out that little had changed over twenty years. The DiGiorgios were and are welcoming hosts. Giulia Orazi makes me feel better every single time we talk. The day I met Ettore Santi in Shanghai, my life changed. I will never feel alone again.

I am sitting on the sofa, and my dog, Maddie, is chewing her rope next to me. The ice-cream truck is outside, playing its familiar jingle that I thought I hated but am now singing to myself. It is one of those perfect winter LA days when the sun brushes us all.

It was a long journey, but I am now home. Steven Weiss Samols, you are home.

Bibliography

Adams, J. A. 1991. *The American Amusement Park Industry: A History of Technology and Thrills.* Boston: Twayne.

Amin, A. 2008. "Collective Culture and Urban Public Space." *City* 12 (1): 5–24.

Anagost, A. 1993. "The Nationscape: Movement in the Field of Vision." *Position* 1 (3): 585–605.

Anderson, E. 2011. *The Cosmopolitan Canopy: Race and Civility in Everyday Life.* New York: Norton.

Arefi, M. 1999. "Nonplace and Placelessness as Narratives of Loss: Rethinking the Notion of Place." *Journal of Urban Design*: 179–93.

Auge, M. 1995. *Non-Places: Introduction to an Anthropology of Supermodernity.* London: Verso.

Bagnall, G. 1996. "Consuming the Past." *Sociological Review* 1: 227–47.

———. 2003. "Performance and Performativity at Heritage Sites." *Museum and Society* 1 (2): 87–103.

Banerjee, T. 2001. "The Future of Public Space: Beyond Invented Streets and Reinvented Places." *Journal of the American Planning Association* 67 (1): 9–24.

Banerjee, T., and A. Loukaitou-Sideris. 2013. "Suspicion, Surveillance, and Safety: A New Imperative for Public Space?" In *Policy, Planning, and People: Promoting Justice in Urban Development*, ed. N. Carmon and S. Fainstein, 337–55. Philadelphia: University of Pennsylvania Press.

Banet-Weiser, S. 2012. *Authentic™: The Politics of Ambivalence in a Brand Culture*. New York: NYU Press.

Baudrillard, J. 1983. *Simulations*. New York: Semiotext(e).

———. 1994. *Simulacra and Simulation*. Ann Arbor: University of Michigan Press.

Beardsworth, A., and A. Bryman. 1999. "Late Modernity and the Dynamics of Quasification: The Case of the Themed Restaurant." *Sociological Review* 47 (2): 228–57.

Bendix, R. 1997. *In Search of Authenticity: The Formation of Folklore Studies*. Madison: University of Wisconsin Press.

Benjamin, W. 2008 (1936). *The Work of Art in the Age of Mechanical Reproduction*. London: Penguin.

Berman, M. 1970. *The Politics of Authenticity*. London: Verso.

Bickers, R., and J. Wasserstrom. 1995. "Shanghai's 'Dogs and Chinese Not Admitted' Sign: Legend, History, and Contemporary Symbol." *China Quarterly* 142:444–466.

Blomley, N. 2007. "How to Turn a Beggar into a Bus Stop: Law, Traffic, and the Function of the Place." *Urban Studies* 44 (9): 1697–712.

Boddy, T. 1992. "Underground and Overhead, Building the Analogous City." In *Variations on a Theme Park: The New American City and the End of Public Space*, ed. M. Sorkin, 123–153. New York: Hill and Wang.

Bosker, B. 2013. *Original Copies: Architectural Mimicry in Contemporary China*. Honolulu: University of Hawai'i Press.

Bourdieu, P. 1984. *Distinction: A Social Critique of the Judgement of Taste*. London: Routledge.

Boyer, C. 1993. "The City of Illusion: New York's Public Places." In *The Restless Urban Landscape*, ed. P. L. Knox, 111–26. Englewood Cliffs, NJ: Prentice Hall.

Brandi, C. 2005 (1963). *Theory of Restoration*. Rome: Nardini.

Bromley, R. D. 1998. "Informal Commerce: Expansion and Exclusion in the Historic Centre of the Latin American City." *International Journal of Urban and Regional Research*: 245–263.

Brown-Saracino, J. 2009. *A Neighborhood That Never Changes: Gentrification, Social Preservation, and the Search for Authenticity.* Chicago: University of Chicago Press.

Bruner, E. M. 2001. "The Maasai and the Lion King: Authenticity, Nationalism, and Globalization in African Tourism." *American Ethnologist* 28 (4): 881–908.

Bryman, A. 1995. *Disney and His Worlds.* New York: Routledge.

———. 2004. *The Disneyization of Society.* London: Sage.

Campanella, T. 2008. "Theme Parks and the Landscape of Consumption." In *The Concrete Dragon: China's Urban Revolution and What It Means for the World,* 241–79. New York: Princeton Architectural Press.

Carmona, M. 2010. "Contemporary Public Space: Critique and Classification, Part One: Critique." *Journal of Urban Design* 15 (1): 123–48.

Çelik, Z., and L. Kinney. 1990. "Ethnography and Exhibitions at the Expositions Universelles." *Assemblage* 13: 34–59.

Certeau de, M. 1980 (1984). *The Practice of Everyday Life.* Berkeley: University of California Press.

Chase, J., M. Crawford, and J. Kaliski. 1999. *Everyday Urbanism.* New York: Monacelli.

Chen, X. 2009. "Introduction." In *Rising Shanghai, State Power, and Local Transformation in a Global Megacity,* ed. C. Xinangming, xv–xxii. Minneapolis: University of Minnesota.

Chen, X., L. Wang, and R. Kundu. 2009. "Localizing the Production of Global Cities: A Comparison of New Town Developments around Shanghai and Kolkata." *City and Community* 8 (4): 433–65.

Clausen, M. 1985. "The Department Store: Development of the Type." *Journal of Architectural Education* 39 (1): 20–29.

Cohen, E. 1988. "Authenticity and Commodization in Tourism." *Annals of Tourism Research* 15: 351–86.

Corbey, R. 1993. "Ethnographic Showcases." *Cultural Anthropology* 8 (3): 338–69.

Cosgrove, D. 1985. "Prospect, Perspective, and the Evolution of the Landscape Idea." *Transactions, Institute of British Geographers.*

Crawford, M. 1995. "Contesting the Public Realm: Struggles over Public Space in Los Angeles." *Journal of Architectural Education* 49 (1): 4–9.

———. 1999. "Introduction." In *Everyday Urbanism*, ed. L. Chase and M. K. Crawford, 6–11. New York: Monacelli.

Cresswell, T. 1996. *In Place/Out of Place: Geography, Ideology, and Transgression*. Minneapolis: University of Minnesota Press.

Cross, J. C., and A. Morales. 2007. *Street Entrepreneurs: People, Place, and Politics in Local and Global Perspective*. London: Rouledge.

Crossa, V. 2009. "Resisting the Entrepreneurial City: Street Vendors' Struggle in Mexico City's Historic Center." *International Journal of Urban and Regional Research* 33: 43–63.

Davis, D. 2000. *The Consumer Revolution in Urban China*. Berkeley: University of California Press.

Davis, M. 1990. *City of Quartz*. London: Verso.

Davis, S. 1996. "The Theme Park, Global Industry, and Cultural Form." *Media, Culture, and Society* 18: 399–422.

Den Hartog, H. 2010. *Shanghai New Towns: Searching for Community and Identity in a Sprawling Metropolis*. Rotterdam: 010.

Denison, E. 2017. *Architecture and the Landscape of Modernity in China before 1949*. London: Routledge.

Denong, Z. 2001. *A History of Modern Chinese Architecture*. Tianjin: Tianjin Science and Technology Press.

Dovey, K. 2010. *Becoming Places: Urbanism/Architecture/Identity/Power*. New York: Routledge.

Eco, U. 1986. *Travels in Hyperreality: Essays*. San Diego, CA: HBJ.

Endersor, T. 2001. "Performing Tourism, Staging Tourism: (Re)producing Tourist Space and Practice." *Tourist Studies* 1 (1): 59–81.

Favro, D. 1994. "The Street Trumphant: The Urban Impact of Roman Trumphal Parades." In *Streets: Critical Perspectives on Public Space*, ed. Z. Çelik, D. Favro, and R. Ingersoll, 151–64). Berkeley: University of California Press.

Feng, J., F. Wang, and Y. Zhou. 2009. "The Spatial Restructuring of Population in Metropolitan Beijing: Toward Polycentricity in the Post-Reform Era." *Urban Geography* 30 (7): 779–802.

Fincher, R. 2003. "Planning for Cities of Diversity, Difference, and Encounter." *Australian Planner* 40 (1): 55–58.

Fincher, R., and J. Jacobs. 1998. *Cities of Difference*. New York: Guilford.

Fiske, J. 1989. *Understanding Popular Culture.* New York: Routledge.

Fiske, J. 2000. "Shopping for Pleasure: Malls, Power, and Resistance." In *The Consumer Society Reader,* ed. J. B. Schor and D. B. Holt, 306–28. New York: New Press.

Fong, W. 1962. "The Problem of Forgeries in Chinese Painting. Part One." *Artibus Asiae* 25 (2/3): 95–119, 121–40.

Francaviglia, R. 1981. "Main Street USA: A Comparison/Contrast of Streetscapes in Disneyland and Walt Disney World." *Journal of Popular Culture* 15 (1): 141–56.

Frantz, D. 1999. *Celebration, U.S.A.: Living in Disney's Brave New Town.* New York: Henry Holt.

Fraser, D. 2000. "Inventing Oasis, Luxury Housing Advertisements, and Reconfiguring Domestic Space in Shanghai." In *The Consumer Revolution in Urban China,* ed. D. Davis, 25–53. Berkeley: University of California Press.

Fraser, N. 1990. "Rethinking the Public Sphere." *Social Text:* 56–80.

Friedman, J., and M. Douglass. 1998. "Introduction." In *Cities for Citizens,* ed. M. Douglass and J. Friedman, 1–8. Chichester: J. Wiley.

Gilmore, J., and J. Pine. 2007. *Authenticity: What Consumers Really Want.* Boston: Harvard Business School Press.

Giroir, G. 2006. "A Globalized Golden Ghetto in a Chinese Garden, the Fontainbleau Villas in Shanghai." In *Globalization and the Chinese City,* ed. W. F. Long, 191–208. Oxon: Routledge.

Goldberger, P. 1972. "Mickey Mouse Teaches the Architects." *New York Times,* October 22.

———. 1989. "Why Design Can't Transform Cities." *New York Times,* June 25.

Gottdiener, M. 1985. *The Social Production of Urban Space.* Austin: University of Texas Press.

———. 1997. *The Theming of America.* Oxford: Westview.

Gottdiener, M., and A. P. Lagopoulos. 1986. *The City and the Sign: An Introduction to Urban Semiotics.* New York: Columbia University Press.

Gramsci, A. 1977 (1929). *Quaderni del carcere.* Torino: Einaudi.

Greenspan, A. 2014. *Shanghai Future: Modernity Remade.* New York: Oxford University Press.

Haley, P., and R. Upton. 2010. *Crossing Borders: International Exchange and Planning Practices.* New York: Routledge.

Hannigan, J. 1998. *Fantasy City: Pleasure and Profit in the Postmodern Metropolis.* New York: Routledge.

———. 2010. "Themed Environments." In *Encyclopedia of Urban Studies*, 806–10. Thousand Oaks, CA: Sage.

Harvey, D. 1989. *The Condition of Postmodernity: An Enquiry into the Origins of Cultural Change.* Oxford: Blackwell.

———. 1990. "Between Space and Time: Reflections on the Geographical Imagination." *Annals of the Association of American Geographers* 80 (3): 418–34.

Harwood, E. 2002. "Rhetoric, Authenticity, and Reception: The Eighteenth-Century Landsape Garden, the Modern Theme Park, and Their Audiences." In *Theme Park Landscapes: Antecedents and Variations*, ed. T. Young and R. Riley, 49–68. Washington, DC: Dumbarton Oaks.

Hassenpflug, D. 2008. *The Urban Code of China.* Basel: Birkhäuser.

Hay, J. 1983. "Values and History in Chinese Painting, I: Hsieh Ho Revisited." *RES: Anthropology and Aesthetics*: 72–111.

Heidegger, M. 1996 (1927). *Being and Time.* Albany: State University of New York Press.

Henningsen, L. 2012. "Individualism for the Masses? Coffee Consumption and the Chinese Middle Class' Search for Authenticity." *Inter-Asia Cultural Studies* 13 (3): 408–427.

Henriot, C., and M. Minost. 2017. "Thames Town, an English Cliché: The Urban Production and Social Construction of a District Featuring Western-Style Architecture in Shanghai." *China Perspectives* 1: 79–86.

Hewitt, D. 2007. *China: Getting Rich First, a Modern Social History.* New York: Pegasus.

Holden-Platt, K. 2012. "Copycat Architects in China Take Aim at the Stars." *Spiegel*, December 28.

Holtorf, C. 2005. *From Stonehenge to Las Vegas: Archaeology as Popular Culture.* Walnut Creek, CA: Altamira.

———. 2009. "On the Possibility of Time Travel." *Lund Archaeological Review*: 31–41.

———. 2013. "On Pastness: A Reconsideration of Materiality in Archaeological Object Authenticity." *Anthropological Quarterly* 86 (2): 427–43.

Horkeimer, M., and T. Adorno. 2002 (1944). *Dialectic of Enlightenment.* Stanford, CA: Stanford University Press.

Huxtable, A. L. 1997. *The Unreal America: Architecture and Illusion*. New York: New Press.

Icomos. 1964. *Venice Charter of Restoration*. Venice.

———. 1994. *The Nara Document on Authenticity*. Paris: International Council for Monuments.

Ito, N. 1995. "<HS>'Authenticity' Inherent in Cultural Heritage in Asia and Japan." In *Nara Conference on Authenticity*, ed. K. Larsen, 17–34). Paris: UNESCO.

Jameson, F. 1991. *Postmodernism, or the Cultural Logic of Late Capitalism*. Durham, NC: Duke University Press.

Jencks, C. 1991. *The Language of Post-Modern Architecture*. New York: Rizzoli.

Jive´n, G., and P. J. Larkham. 2003. "Sense of Place, Authenticity, and Character: A Commentary." *Journal of Urban Design* 8 (1): 67–81.

Jokilehto, J. 1995. "Authenticity, a General Framework for the Concept." In *Nara Conference on Authenticity, Proceedings*, ed. K. Larsen, 19–34. Paris: UNESCO.

Jones, S. 2010. "Negotiating Authentic Objects and Authentic Selves, Beyond the Deconstruction of Authenticity." *Journal of Material Culture* 15 (2): 181–203.

Judd, D. 1999. "Constructing the Tourist Bubble." In *The Tourist City*, ed. D. Judd and S. Fainstein, 35–53. New Haven, CT: Yale University Press.

———. 2008. "Visitors and the Spatial Ecology of the City." In *Cities and Visitors: Regulating People, Markets, and City Space*, ed. L. Hoffman and S. S. Fainstein, 23–38. Hoboken, NJ: John Wiley & Sons.

Judd, D., and S. Fainstein. 1999. *The Tourist City*. New Haven, CT: Yale University Press.

Kim, A. M. 2015. *Sidewalk City: Remapping Public Space in Ho Chi Minh City*. Chicago: University of Chicago Press.

King, M. J. 1981. "Disneyland and Walt Disney World: Traditional Values in Futuristic Form." *Journal of Popular Culture* 15 (1): 116–40.

Kirshenblatt-Gimblett, B. 2004. "Intangible Heritage as Metacultural Production." *Museum* 56 (1/2): 52–65.

Klingmann, A. 2007. *Brandscapes: Architecture in the Experience Economy*. Cambridge, MA: MIT Press.

Kloet, J., and L. Scheen. 2013. "Pudong: The Shanzhai Global City." *European Journal of Cultural Studies* 16 (6): 692–709.

Knudsen, B. T., and A. M. Waade. 2010. "Performative Authenticty in Tourism and Spatial Experience: Rethinking the Relations between Travel, Place, and Emotion." In *Re-Investing Authenticity, Tourism, Place, and Emotions*, ed. B. T. Knudsen and A. M. Waade, 1–22. Bristol: Channel View.

Koenig, D. 1994. *Mouse Tales. A Behind-the-Ears Look at Disneyland.* Irvine, CA: Bonaventure.

Kohn, M. 2010. *Brave New Neighborhoods: The Privatization of Public Space.* New York: Routledge.

Kuutma, K. 2015. "From Folklore to Intangible Heritage." In *A Companion to Heritage Studies*, ed. C. M. Loga, 41–54. Malden, MA: Wiley-Blackwell.

Lang, J. 2011. "City Branding." In *Companion to Urban Design*, ed. T. Banerjee and A. Loukaitou-Sideris, 541–51. London : Routledge.

Larsen, K. E. 1995. *Nara Conference on Authenticity in Relation to the World Heritage Convention, Nara, Japan, 1–6 November 1994: Proceedings.* Paris: UNESCO World Heritage Centre.

Lefebvre, H. 1991 (1974). *The Production of Space.* Oxford: Blackwell.

Lefebvre, H. 1996 (1968). "The Right to the City." In *Writings on Cities*, ed. E. Kofman and E. Lebas. Cambridge: Wiley-Blackwell.

Lerner, P. F. 2015. *The Consuming Temple: Jews, Department Stores, and the Consumer Revolution in Germany, 1880–1940.* Ithaca, NY: Cornell University Press.

Li, J., and J. Yang. 2007. "Chinese Theme Park's Management Innovation against an Information Age Background." *Human Geography* 27 (3): 505–508.

Li, X. 2006. "In Search of Quality." *Volume* 2: 98.

———. 2008. "<HS>'Make-the-Most-of-It' Architecture: Young Architects and Chinese Tactics." *City: Analysis of Urban Trends, Culture, Theory, Policy, Action* 12 (2): 226–36.

———. 2010. "Heterotopias: Themed Spaces in Shanghai and Los Angeles." In *Shanghai New Towns: Searching for Community and Identity in a Sprawling Metropolis*, ed. H. Den Hartog, 224–38. Rotterdam: 010.

———. 2015. "Building Shanghai: Transformation of a Modern City."
Public lecture at the conference Shanghai: A (Self)Portrait,
May 26. M. F. Piazzoni, interviewer.

Li, X., and X. Zhang. 2008. "From Lilong to International
Community." In *Shanghai Transforming: The Changing
Physical, Economic, Social, and Environmental Conditions
of a Global Metropolis*, ed. I. Gil, 204–11. Barcelona: Actar.

Li, Z. 2010. *In Search of Paradise: Middle-Class Living in a
Chinese Metropolis*. Ithaca, NY: Cornell University Press.

Lin, G. C. 2007. "Chinese Urbanism in Question: State, Society, and
the Reproduction of Urban Spaces." *Urban Geography* 28 (1):
7–29.

Liu, S. 2011. "The Chinese Theme Parks Go to Where?" *Chinese
Social Science Today*, July 19.

Loukaitou-Sideris, A. 2012. "Addressing the Challenges of Urban
Landscapes: Normative Goals for Urban Design." *Journal of
Urban Design* 17 (4): 467–84.

Loukaitou-Sideris, A., and T. Banerjee. 1998. *Urban Design
Downtown Poetics and Politics of Form*. Berkeley: University
of California Press.

Low, S. 1996. "Spatializing Culture: The Social Production and
Social Construction of Public Space in Costa Rica." *American
Ethnologist* 23 (4): 861–79.

Lowenthal, D. 2002. "The Past as a Theme Park." In *Theme Park
Landscapes: Antecedents and Variations*, ed. T. Young and
R. Riley, 11–24. Washington, DC: Dumbarton Oaks.

Lu, S., X. Yang, and W. Tang. 2011. "On the Tourist Impact of Urban
Residents' Perceptions and Attitude on the Mega Theme Parks:
A Case Study of Fangtaworld Adventure in Wuhu City."
Tourism Tribune 26 (8): 45–52.

Lukas, S. A. 2007. *The Themed Space: Locating Culture, Nation,
and Self*. Lanham, MD: Lexington.

———. 2013. *The Immersive Worlds Handbook: Designing Theme
Parks and Consumer Spaces*. Burlington: Focal.

Madanipour, A. 2006. "Roles and Challenges of Urban Design."
Journal of Urban Design 11 (2): 173–93.

MacCannel, D. 1973. "Staged Authenticity: Arrangements of Social
Space in Tourist Settings." *American Journal of Sociology* 79
(3): 589–603.

———. 1976. *The Tourist: A New Theory for the Leisure Class.* New York: Schocken.

Man, J. 2011. *China's Housing Reforms and Outcomes.* Cambridge: University of Cambridge Press.

Mannheim, S. 2002. *Walt Disney and the Quest for Community.* Burlington: Ashgate.

Marling, K. A. 1997. "Imagineering the Disney Theme Park." In *Designing Disney's Theme Parks: The Architecture of Reassurance,* ed. K. A. Marling, 29–178. Montreal: Centre canadien d'architecture/Canadian Centre for Architecture.

McLeod, M. 1989. "Architecture and Politics in the Reagan Era: From Postmodernism to Deconstructivism." *Assemblage* 8: 22–59.

Miller Disney, D. 1956. *The Story of Walt Disney.* New York: Dell.

Mitchell, D. 2003. *The Right to the City: Social Justice and the Fight for Public Space.* New York: Guilford.

Moore, C. 2004 (1972). "You Have to Pay for the Public Life." In *You Have to Pay for the Public Life: Selected Essays of Charles W. Moore,* ed. K. P. Keim, 115–37. Cambridge, MA: MIT Press.

Munjeri, D. 2004. "Tangible and Intangible Heritage: From Difference to Convergence." *Museum International* 56 (1/2): 12–20.

Oakes, T. 2006. "The Village as a Theme Park: Mimesis and Authenticity in Chinese Tourism." In *Translocal China: Linkages, Identities, and the Reimagining of Space,* ed. T. Oakes and L. Schein, 166–92. New York: Routledge.

Olds, K. 2004. *Globalization and Urban Change: Capital, Culture, and Pacific Rim Mega-Projects.* Oxford: Oxford University Press.

Ottinger, D. 2010. "Dreamlands, Introduction." In *Dreamlands,* by Q. Bajac and D. Ottinger, 17–35. Paris: Centre Pompidou.

Ouf, A. M. 2001. "Authenticity and the Sense of Place in Urban Design." *Journal of Urban Design* 6 (1): 73–86.

Pearce, P. L. and G. Moscardo. 1986. "The Concept of Authenticity in Tourist Experiences." *Australian and New Zealand Journal of Sociology* 22: 121–32.

Peattie, L. 1999. "Convivial Cities." In *Cities for Citizens,* ed. M. Douglass and J. Friedmann, 247–53. Chichester: Wiley.

Peiss, K. L. 1986. *Cheap Amusements: Working Women and Leisure in Turn-of-the-Century New York.* Philadelphia: Temple University Press.

Piazzoni, M. F., and T. Banerjee. 2017. "Mimicry in Design: The Urban Form of Development." *Journal of Urban Design*: 1–17.

Pike, D. L. 2005. "The Disney World Underground." *Space and Culture* 8 (47): 47–65.

Pow, C. P. 2009. *Gated Communities in China: Class, Privilege, and the Moral Politics of the Good Life*. London: Routledge.

Purcell, M. 2003. "Citizenship and the Right to the Global City: Reimagining the Capitalist World Order." *International Journal of Urban and Regional Research* 27 (3): 564–90.

Ramaswamy, S. 2014. "The Work of Vision in the Age of European Empires." In *Empires of Vision*, by M. Jay and S. Ramaswamy, 1–22. Durham, NC: Duke University Press.

Rath, J. 2007. *Tourism Ethnic Diversity and the City*. New York: Routledge.

Redfoot, D. 1984. "Touristic Authenticity, Touristic Angst, and Modern Reality." *Qualitative Sociology* 7 (4): 291–309.

Ren, X. 2010. *Building Globalization*. Chicago: University of Chicago Press.

Rice, P. 2012. "Interview with the Architect-in-Chief of Thames Town, for Atkins." October 18. M. F. Piazzoni, interviewer.

Rickly-Boyd, J. 2013. "Existential Authenticity: Place Matters." *Tourism Geographies* 15 (4): 680–86.

Ritzer, G. 1999. *Enchanting a Disenchanted World: Revolutionizing the Means of Consumption*. Thousand Oaks, CA: Pine Forge.

———. 2003. "Islands of the Living Dead: The Social Geography of McDonaldization." *American Behavioral Scientist* 47 (2): 119–36.

Rojek, C. 2000. *Leisure and Culture*. London: Macmillan.

Rosenthal, E. 2003. "North of Beijing, California Dreams Come True." *New York Times*, February 3.

Ross, A. 1999. *The Celebration Chronicles: Life, Liberty, and the Pursuit of Property Value in Disney's New Town*. New York: Ballantine.

Rossi, A. 1990. *Autobiografia Scientifica*. Parma: Pratiche.

Rowe, P., and S. Kuan. 2004. *Architectural Encounters with Essence and Form in Modern China*. Cambridge, MA: MIT Press.

Ryckmans, P. 2008 (1989). "The Chinese Attitude towards the Past." *China Heritage Quarterly*: 1–16.

Sandercock, L. 1998. "The Death of Modernist Planning: Radical Praxis for a Postmodern Age." In *Cities for Citizens*, ed. M. Douglass and J. Friedman, 163–84. Chichester: John Wiley.

Santi, E. 2017. "Uncertainty and Design Practice in China: The 'Apparatus' of Shanghai Experimental Architecture." *Journal of Architecture and Urbanism* 41 (2): 120–28.

Sassen, S. 2009. "The Global City Perspective, Theoretical Implication for Shanghai." In *Shanghai Rising: State Power and Local Transformations in a Global Megacity*, ed. Xinangming Chen, 3–29. Minneapolis: University of Minnesota Press.

Savitch, H., and P. B. Kantor. 2002. *Cities in the International Marketplace: The Political Economy of Urban Development in North America and Western Europe*. Princeton, NJ: Princeton University Press.

Schwartz, V. R. 2003. *Spectacular Realities: Early Mass Culture in Fin-de-Siècle Paris*. Berkeley: University of California Press.

Sennett, R. 1970. *Uses of Disorder*. New York: Knopf.

———. 1977. *The Fall of Public Man*. New York: Knopf.

Shaw, S., S. Bagwell, and J. Karmowska. 2004. "Ethnoscapes as Spectacle: Reimaging Multicultural Districts as New Destinations for Leisure and Tourism Consumption." *Urban Studies* 40 (1): 1983–2000.

Shen, J. 2011. "Suburban Development in Shanghai: A Case of Songjiang." PhD diss., School of City and Regional Planning, Cardiff University, http://orca.cf.ac.uk/23846/.

Shen, J. and F. Wu. 2011. "Restless Urban Landscapes in China: A Case Study of Three Projects in Shanghai." *Journal of Urban Affairs* 34 (3): 255–77.

Shen, J., and F. Wu. 2013. "Moving to the Suburbs: Demand-Side Driving Forces of Suburban Growth in China." *Environment and Planning A* 45: 1823–44.

Shenker, H. 2002. "Pleasure Gardens, Theme Park, and the Pictoresque." In *Theme Park Landscapes: Antecedents and Variations*, ed. T. Young and R. Riley, 69–90. Washington, DC: Dumbarton Oaks.

Shepard, W. 2016. "Why China Keeps Building So Many Western-Style Copycat Towns." *Forbes*, January 19.

Shien, Z., H. L. Zhang, and H. Zhang. 2014. "Variations on a Theme Park in Contemporary China." *Asia Pacific World* 5 (2): 101–22.

Silbergeld, J. 2013. "Foreword." In *Original Copies: Architectural Mimicry in Contemporary China,* ed. B. Bianka, vii–ix). Honolulu: University of Hawai'i Press.

Sloane, D. C., and B. Conant Sloane. 2003. *Medicine Moves to the Mall.* Baltimore, MD: Johns Hopkins University Press.

Smith, L., and G. Campbel. 2015. "The Elephant in the Room: Heritage, Affect, and Emotion." In *Heritage Regimes and the State,* ed. R. Bendix, A. Eggert, and A. Peselmann, 21–36. Goettingen: University of Goettingen Press.

Soja, E. W. 1989. *Postmodern Geographies: The Reassertion of Space in Critical Social Theory.* London: Verso.

———. 1992. "Inside Exopolis: Scenes from Orange County." In *Variations on a Theme Park: The New American City and the End of Public Space,* ed. M. Sorkin, 94–122. New York: Hill and Wang.

Sorkin, M. 1992. *Variations on a Theme Park: The New American City and the End of Public Space.* New York: Hill and Wang.

Stille, A. 2002. *The Future of the Past.* New York: Picador.

Stovel, H. 1995. "Working Towards the Nara Document." In *Nara Conference on Authenticity in Relation to the World Heritage Convention,* ed. K. E. Larsen, 33–37. Paris: UNESCO.

Tomba, L. 2004. "Creating an Urban Middle Class, Social Engineering in Beijing." *China Journal* 51: 1–26.

Thompson, W. I. 1971. *At the Edge of History and Passages about Earth.* New York: Harper and Row.

Trilling, L. 1972. *Sincerity and Authenticity.* Oxford: Oxford University Press.

Tse, E., Y. Huang, and K. Ma. 2009. *Shan Zhai: A Chinese Phenomenon.* London: Booz.

UNESCO. 2003. *Convention for the Safeguarding of the Intangible Cultural Heritage.* Paris: UNESCO.

Vannini, P. 2011. "Authenticity." In *Encyclopedia of Consumer Culture,* ed. D. Southerton, 74–76. Thousand Oaks, CA: SAGE.

Viladas, P. 1988. "Mickey the Talent Scout." *Progressive Architecture* 68: 104–5.

Wakeman, F. 1995. *Policing Shanghai, 1927–1937.* Berkeley: University of California Press.

Wallace, M. 1985. "Mickey Mouse History: Portraying the Past at Disney World." *Radical History Review* 32: 33–57.

Wang, L., R. Kundu, and X. Chen. 2010. "Building for What and Whom? New Town Development as Planned Suburbanization in China and India." *Research in Urban Sociology* 10: 319–45.

Wang, N. 1999. "Rethinking Authenticity in Tourism Experience." *Annals of Tourism Research* 26 (2): 349–70.

Wang, S. W. 2011. "The Evolution of Housing Renewal in Shanghai, 1990–2010: A Socially Conscious Entrepreneurial City?" *International Design of Housing Policy* 11 (1): 51–56.

Warren, S. 1994. "Disneyfication of the Metropolis: Popular Resistance in Seattle." *Journal of Urban Affairs* 16 (2): 89–107.

———. 1999. "Cultural Contestation at Disneyland Paris." In *Leisure/Tourism Geographies: Practices and Geographical Knowledge*, ed. D. Crouch, 109–25. London: Routledge.

———. 2005. "Saying No to Disney: Disney Demise in Four American Cities." In *Rethinking Disney: Private Control, Public Dimension*, ed. M. Budd and M. Kirch, 231–59. Middletown, CT: Wesleyan University Press.

Weiler, K. 2016. "Aspects of Architectural Authenticity in Chinese Heritage Theme Parks." In *Authenticity in Architectural Heritage Conservation: Discourses, Opinions, Experiences in Europe, South and East Asia*, ed. K. Weiler and N. Gutschow, 219–46. New York: Springer.

Whyte, W. 1998. *City: Rediscovering the Center*. Doubleday.

Wong, W. 2013. *Van Gogh on Demand: China and the Readymade*. Chicago: University of Chicago Press.

Wu, B.-H., and X.-B. Xu. 2010. "Tourism-Oriented Land Development (TOLD): A New Pattern of Tourism–Real Estate Development in China." *Tourism Tribune*.

Wu, F. L. 2000. "The Global and Local Dimensions of Place-Making: Remaking Shanghai as a World City." *Urban Studies* 37 (8): 1359–77.

———. 2003. "The (Post-)Socialist Entrepreneurial City as a State Project: Shanghai's Reglobalization in Question." *Urban Studies* 40 (9): 1673–98.

———. 2005. "Rediscovering the 'Gate' under Market Transition: From Work-Unit Compounds to Commodity Housing Enclaves." *Housing Studies* 20: 235–54.

———. 2006. "Transplanting Cityscapes: Townhouses and Gated Community." In *Globalization and the Chinese City*, ed. F. L. Wu, 190–207. Oxon: Routledge.

———. 2009. "Neourbanism in the Making under China's Market Transition." *City* 13 (4): 418–32.

———. 2010. "Gated and Packaged Suburbia: Packaging and Branding Chinese Suburban Residential Development." *Cities* 27 (5): 385–96.

Xue, C. Q. 2006. *Building a Revolution: Chinese Architecture since 1980*. Hong Kong: Hong Kong University Press.

Xue, C. Q., and M. Zhou. 2007. "Importation and Adaptation: Building One City and Nine Towns in Shanghai: A Case Study of Vittorio Gregotti's Plan of Pujiang Town." *Urban Design International*: 21–40.

Young, I. M. 1989. "Polity and Group Difference: A Critique of the Ideal of Universal Citizenship." *Ethics* 99 (2): 250–74.

Young, T. 2002. "Grounding the Myth: Theme Park Landscapes in an Era of Commerce and Nationalism." In *Theme Park Landscapes*, by T. Young and R. Riley, 1–10. Washington, DC: Dumbarton Oaks.

Yue, W., Y. Liu, and P. Fan. 2010. "Polycentric Urban Development: The Case of Hangzhou." *Environment and Planning A*: 563–577.

Yung, H. C. 2006. "The Necessity of Banality." *Volume*: 86–89.

Zhang, W., and S. Shan. 2016. "The Theme Park Industry in China: A Research Review." *Cogent Social Sciences* 2: 1–17.

Zhong, X., and X. Chen. 2017. "Demolition, Rehabilitation, and Conservation: Heritage in Shanghai's Urban Regeneration, 1990–2015." *Journal of Architecture and Urbanism* 41 (2): 82–91.

Zhu, J. 2005. "Criticality in between China and the West." *Journal of Architecture*: 479–98.

Zhu, Y. 2012. "Performing Heritage: Rethinking Authenticty in Tourism." *Annals of Tourism Research* 39 (3): 1495–1513.

———. 2016. "Authenticity and Heritage Conservation in China: Translation, Interpretation, Practices." In *Authenticity in Architectural Heritage Conservation: Discourses, Opinions, Experiences in Europe, South and East Asia*, ed. K. Weiler and N. Gutschow, 187–200. New York: Springer.

Zou, D. 2001. *A History of Modern Chinese Architecture*. Tianjin: Tianjin Press of Science and Technology.

Zukin, S. 1991. *Landscapes of Power: From Detroit to Disney World*. Berkeley: University of California Press.

———. 1995. *The Cultures of Cities*. Malden, MA: Blackwell.

———. 2008. "Consuming Authenticity: From Outposts of Difference to Means of Exclusion." *Cultural Studies* 22:724–48.

———. 2009. "Changing Landscapes of Power: Opulence and the Urge for Authenticity." *International Journal of Urban and Regional Research* 33 (2): 543–33.

———. 2010. *Naked City: The Death and Life of Authentic Urban Places.* Oxford: Oxford University Press.

Reviews of Maria Francesca Piazzoni's
THE REAL FAKE

REVIEWERS: BRUCE O'NEILL, SAINT LOUIS
UNIVERSITY
LYN MACGREGOR, UNIVERSITY OF WISCONSIN

Sandwiches and case studies suffer from the same problem: what to wrap around all that really good meat. The solution to this problem, one that Piazzoni was encouraged to use by both reviewers, was to add even more meat and find an easier-to-swallow set of ideas to wrap around it.

Scholars-in-the-making such as Piazzoni are inclined to use the thickest and freshest bread around, thinking that fancier theories will make the story they're telling more compelling. They don't. Adding more meat does.

In Piazzoni's case, and others like it, the addition of more stories lets the author and reader draw an even bolder circle around lessons that might otherwise have been lost or overwhelmed by heavier slabs of theoretical dough.

1.   Everyday Chinese people are acquiring middle-class sensibilities and engaging in behavior that can only be described as "bourgeois."

2.   Their public and private lives today are every bit as orderly as the ones they used to lead. But they are built on ideas about individual acquisitiveness and prosperity that wouldn't have been talked about, much less celebrated, a half-century ago.

3.   A little more wealth and individual debt are associated with standards of decorous behavior and class snobbery that are reflected in the very places people live, work, and play.

4.   They are becoming more like us.

I suppose the theme park–like way of life being created in Thames Town could be part of some big fake-out promoted by the Chinese government: a living laboratory of consumer excess that everyone who doesn't live there or play there will see come back to bite the hands of the men, women, and children who do. However, I think that Lewis Mumford got it right when he said that crazy urban places happen when the cuckoo bird of capitalism is allowed to lay a bigger egg than government leaders bargained for or ever imagined possible. Thames Town foreshadows a world in the making every bit as vital and cracked as the one revealed by Dickens' ghosts in the real nineteenth-century London.

Whether Piazzoni sees it this way is irrelevant. All the creative sense she made of the way of life created by the residents of Thames Town—and even the people who drop in for a visit—lets me see it that way. The point, I suppose, is this. There's more than enough good meat in *The Real Fake* to go around, no matter what kind of bread we're inclined to wrap around it. That's the hallmark of a scholar-in-the-making whose work is worth reading and taking seriously.

Daniel J. Monti

Ingram Content Group UK Ltd.
Milton Keynes UK
UKHW022138300323
419440UK00010B/83